POKER:
A WINNER'S GUIDE

Other Books by Andy Nelson

POKER: 101 WAYS TO WIN

POKER: HOLD 'EM, BOOK ONE

POKER: HOLD 'EM, INTERMEDIATE

POKER: HOLD 'EM, ADVANCED

POKER: OMAHA, BOOK ONE

POKER: OMAHA, HIGH/LOW SPLIT, BOOK ONE

POKER: SEVEN-CARD STUD, HIGH/LOW SPLIT, BOOK ONE

POKER: SEVEN-CARD STUD, HIGH/LOW SPLIT, INTERMEDIATE

POKER: SEVEN WAYS TO WIN

POKER: SEVEN MORE WAYS TO WIN

Most Perigee Books are available at special quantity discounts for bulk purchases for sales promotions, premiums, fund-raising or educational use. Special books, or book excerpts, can also be created to fit specific needs.

For details, write: Special Markets: The Berkley Publishing Group, 375 Hudson Street, New York, New York 10014.

POKER:
A WINNER'S
GUIDE

ANDY NELSON

A PERIGEE BOOK

ACKNOWLEDGMENTS

The card illustrations used in this book are images of Bicycle cards, Jumbo Size, #8082. These cards are the registered trademarks of The United States Playing Card Company of Cincinnati, Ohio. Our thanks to that company for allowing us to use these images.

My personal thanks go to many people who have made significant contributions, directly and indirectly, to this book. A special thanks to Steven Divide for reading the manuscript and offering important advice.

A Perigee Book
Published by The Berkley Publishing Group
A division of Penguin Putnam Inc.
375 Hudson Street
New York, NY 10014

Copyright © 1996 by Andy Nelson
Book design by Rhea Braunstein Design
Cover design by James R. Harris
Cover illustration by George Kerrigan

First edition: July 1996

Published simultaneously in Canada.

The Penguin Putnam Inc. World Wide Web site address is
http://www.penguinputnam.com

Library of Congress Cataloging-in-Publication Data

Nelson, Andy.
    Poker : a winner's guide / Andy Nelson.—1st ed.
    p. cm.
    "A Perigee book."
    ISBN 0-399-52212-3
    1. Poker. 2. Gambling. I. Title.
  GV1251.N44   1996
  795.41'2—dc20   95-43071
                                                      CIP

Printed in the United States of America

15 14 13 12 11 10

CONTENTS

INTRODUCTION

I'm going to start off by giving you "the secret" to becoming a winner in poker. Right here in the beginning of the book. Remember this tip. You might not believe this at first, but trust me. I believe that you will agree with me by the end of the book. The secret? *Poker is not a card game, it is a people game played with cards and chips.* There, now you know my secret. With that information fully developed, you can compete with world-class players. Of course, you must begin by mastering the logistics of the game, but keep in mind that your knowledge of people will be the difference between winning and losing. So part of your preparation should be the studying of the trends of the people you play with regularly. When you know what they do in various circumstances, you will be able to take advantage of their habits.

The premise behind this book is to give the recreational poker player the choice to increase or progress beyond his or her current level and move into bigger arenas of poker. If you have so far confined your poker play to family gatherings, or with a few friends on a monthly or weekly basis, you have the opportunity to have some adventure and make some important money in the process.

VIII / ANDY NELSON

But let me make it clear that the intent of this book is *not* to encourage anyone to gamble. I do, however, want to encourage you to grow in your poker knowledge and ability at a pace that is comfortable for you. When you feel you have achieved a certain level of competency, and you feel you are ready for the next step, then you might want to investigate the possibility of moving up. I encourage this only as one would encourage a novice runner to continue to train and develop his muscles and speed. To the runner, I would say that if you follow this course of training, it is possible that you might get hurt. You might fall or suffer an injury that will disable you forever.

Please run and train at your own risk. Expanding your poker abilities is the risk *you* take, but you must be aware that you take that risk as a fully informed person. You can get hurt playing poker. You can lose your money. You could even become addicted. You could lose a fortune playing poker because you cannot control yourself. That is the risk you take all by yourself. True, poker is a skill that you can learn that can provide monetary rewards. However, if you have a predisposition toward addiction, you could be in for trouble.

It takes only a few moments to learn the basics of poker, but it takes a lifetime to learn the intricacies of the game. The attraction of poker is both its simplicity and its complexity. Poker can be extremely profitable, or it can bankrupt you. Perhaps it is this polarity that draws us to the game. Whether you are a newcomer to the game or just trying to polish your skills, I wish you well.

COMMON POKER GAMES

The game of poker became increasingly popular in the nineteenth and twentieth centuries, mostly in America, but exactly where and how it started is unclear. Some have suggested the game was conceived by the merging of two or three European and Middle Eastern games. Poker, as we know it, probably was born in the southern United States, grew into its adolescence on the riverboats along the big rivers and reached adulthood in the wild American west. Some claim the riverboats, like the ones that trolled up and down the Mississippi and Missouri rivers, contributed immensely to the growth of poker. This is most likely true.

Throughout the years, poker has evolved into many forms and variations. The purpose of this section is to give you a brief outline on the most popular poker games played. I'm going to restrict it to the straight poker games, not the ones normally played with several wild cards. This book is, after all, designed for the serious recreational player who desires to advance and learn the intricacies of the game. The intent is to help make the reader more comfortable and confident when he or she sits down to play. The more you know about all the games, the greater your overall knowledge of poker, and the more enjoyment you'll have when you win.

1

FIVE-CARD DRAW POKER

POKER IS A PRAGMATIC GAME. It pits person against person in competitive roles. When the hand is dealt, the challenge to combat is issued. "Come forth and do battle" is the call. Consequently, some descriptions of the different poker games are also pragmatic. Draw poker is named because the contestants draw cards to complete their hands. After the *ante* or *blind* is placed in the pot (and sometimes one or more blinds), each person is dealt five cards face down, one at a time. A blind wager is a designated amount of money placed in the pot before the cards are dealt. Hence the name blind. The blind is sometimes used instead of an ante, which is an amount of money placed by every player before the cards are dealt. The blind is usually placed by the player or players to the left of the dealer or designated dealer. There can be more than one blind, two being usual. The first blind is usually a smaller amount and is called the small blind. The other blind is called the big blind. The blind concept is to start the action and encourage participation. After the cards are dealt, the action begins with the player to the left of the big blind. Each player has the option of calling, raising or folding. After all the other players have acted, the blind can call all bets or raise if they choose. Since the average hand dealt is usually a losing hand, it is common for players in late positions to raise just to force the blinds to fold. There is now a betting round. Beginning at the left of the dealer, each person in turn has the option of *opening* or *passing*. To open means to wager some money. If the game has a certain qualifier like "jacks or better," the opener must have at least a pair of jacks or better to open. Four cards to a flush or four cards to a straight do not qualify for openers in a "jacks or better" game. Obviously, a pair of tens or below does not qualify either.

How the Game Is Played

After the opening wager is placed, each player in turn has the option of *folding, calling* (matching the size of the bet) or *raising* (increasing the size of the bet). If the game is a *limit* game, the opening bet must be the designated amount. If the game is a *no-limit* game, the opening bet can be of any size. In either case, each raise must be at least the size of the original bet. For instance, if the opener bets $5, a raise must be at least $5 more. When a $5 raise is made, the minimum total amount to call is $10.

After all the players have acted to either call or fold, the draw begins. Each player, starting with the person on the dealer's left, asks the dealer for a certain number of cards. The player discards the number of cards he calls for and the dealer gives him that many replacement cards. Each player in turn draws new cards, with the dealer drawing last. As he draws his own cards, he says something like, "The dealer takes two cards." He discards his cards and then deals himself the replacements. (You can draw no cards, if you choose. That is called *standing pat*.)

After the draw is completed, the second betting round begins. The player who opened the original betting begins the action. He or she can check (to pass without putting money in the pot) or bet. Each player, in turn, can check (if there is no previous wager), fold, call or raise. This continues until all the players have acted. Now is the time for the showdown. In order to win the pot, one of two things must happen: a. the player with the best hand must show his or her cards, or b. one player bets and no one calls. If player A says, "I have a straight" and shows the cards to demonstrate his or her straight, the other players who have lesser hands can discard their hands except for the person who opened the betting. If the game has a qualifier like jacks or better, the opener must show the cards that prove he had the right to open.

All other players can *muck* (toss into the discard pile) their hands without showing them to the table if they choose. Most house rules allow anyone active in the pot at the end the privilege of seeing any other hand they choose to look at. If player D wants to see the cards of player C, he simply asks. Then the cards are turned face up for all to see. This is one of the courtesies of poker. All called hands can be shown. Some house rules allow only players active at the end to ask to see a hand. It is common in card rooms and casinos to have the rule that any player may ask to see a called hand. This rule is meant to discourage people from playing partners.

Quite often a Five-Card Draw game is played with the Joker, also called the *Bug*. The Joker is usually considered a limited wild card. The Joker can normally be used in "aces, straights and flushes." It becomes another ace when paired with one or more aces, and it can be any card in a straight or an ace (or any other high card) in a flush.

One example of an excellent draw situation with the Joker is:

This hand can be called a 22-way hand because there are 22 cards that will make a straight flush, flush or straight. There are even more possibilities. Catching any ace will give you a pair of aces, which might defeat someone who opened with jacks, queens or kings and did not improve. This is a good situation to be in.

Here is an example of a 19-way hand:

Three cards will make a straight flush, seven will make an ace-high flush and nine cards will make a straight. There is no doubt, the Joker adds a lot of possibilities to the game.

Differences From Stud Poker

One thing to note and be aware of if you play draw poker is that there are only two betting rounds, compared to four betting rounds in Five-Card Stud and five betting rounds in Seven-Card Stud. Because there are only two betting rounds in draw, there are not nearly as many strategic moves that can be made compared to stud games. Another important difference between stud and draw are the clues you have when you try to determine the strength of an opponent's hand. In draw you get major clues from the way a person bets and the number of cards he or she draws. In stud you have betting clues, plus you see exposed cards. Those exposed cards provide another important source of information for you to coordinate as you make the evaluation of your opponent's strength. These are just a couple of important differences between draw and stud.

Basic Strategy for Straight High Draw

Five-Card Draw is a game of aces! If you can remember that throughout a long session, you will do okay. Many players will call with any pair. That is not you. Do not call an opening wager with any pair less than aces until you become a very experienced player. When you have enough experience you will be able to recognize which players play poor cards. When you have identified these players, in some circumstances you may profitably call with kings. However, be prepared to dump the hand if you do not improve or any of the other players show strength. Again, do not call with a pair of kings, queens or jacks until you have logged a lot of hours at the table. If you are dealt a pair of aces, you can open from any position. You will also make more money with a pair of aces than any other hand for two reasons: Because of the Joker, it is dealt more frequently than any other stronger hand and it will defeat any other pair or any other two pairs if both hands improve to two pairs. Aces is the name of the game in Five-Card Draw.

Sometimes it makes mathematical sense to split the openers, say a pair of queens, to draw to a flush. What a player must do here to prove he or she had the necessary pair, jacks or better, is to announce that he or she is splitting and then place the card face down under a chip or give it to the dealer to set aside. After the betting is complete and the cards shown, this card is turned up to prove the player had the qualifying cards to open the betting.

There are many, many other important strategies to know. In all of these descriptions of the various games, I will only give a tip or two about the game. I strongly urge you to research a lot more before you risk any significant money.

FIVE-CARD LOWBALL DRAW

Lowball draw is an upside-down version of poker. Instead of the best hand, as in regular draw, lowball is a contest to have the *worst hand*. The worst becomes the best. Pretty crazy, huh? Surely there is a message here.

I wish I could simply cut to the chase here and just tell you about lowball, but this description has to take into account different varieties of the game. I will describe two types of lowball.

There are more. Different parts of the country play variations of this fascinating game. In addition, there are quite a number of hybrids that involve betting rules and structures, blinds and ante combinations, etc. Before you play, try to get a good handle on the specific rules used in your area.

As one might expect from the upside-down nature of lowball, the game is wild and crazy. The people who are attracted to lowball love to gamble. They invent regulations that encourage participation. The pots are often huge and the money swings are tremendous. If you like a lot of action, lowball is your game.

Kansas City Lowball

This is real lowball. Another name for this game is Deuce-to-Seven Lowball. That gives you a good idea of what the game is like. In this game the deuce is the lowest card in the deck and straights and flushes count for high, never for low. Contrast this with California Lowball, described below. In Kansas City Lowball the very best (worst) hand is 2-3-4-5-7 with at least two suits. For example, this hand:

beats this flush:

It is important to note that Deuce-to-Seven Lowball is seldom, if ever played with the Joker. Let me point out some other examples:

This hand . . .

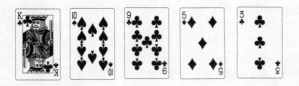

beats this hand . . .

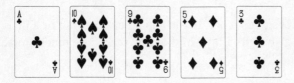

This hand . . .

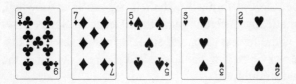

beats this hand . . .

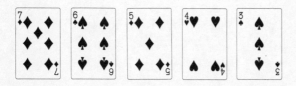

Just remember the ace is always high, the deuce is the low card, straights and flushes always count for high. Deuce-to-Seven is really the purest example of the worst hands in poker. One significant piece of advice to keep in mind in Deuce-to-Seven Lowball is: Seldom draw to an outside straight in late position (last or almost last to act) and *never* from early position. If you have a hand like this:

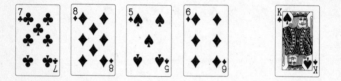

Seldom, if ever, call a bet. If you should catch a four or a nine, you will have a straight. Either of those two cards are much worse than a face card.

California Lowball

Another name for California Lowball is Ace-to-Five Lowball. This is a dramatically different game than Deuce-to-Seven Lowball. The ace is the lowest card, and straights and flushes are disregarded. The very best low hand is called a *wheel,* which is the lowest possible straight, or:

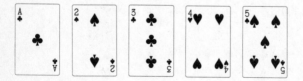

Usually, the Joker is used in California Lowball and can be used as any card you choose.

It is difficult to overstate the importance of the Joker. In some circumstances, if you have the Joker, you almost *double* your chances of drawing a card that will make your hand a good one. Compare this hand which gives you eight chances to make a wheel (any three or any four):

to this hand where you have five chances to make a wheel:

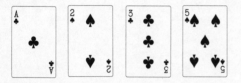

As you know, the wheel is unbeatable in lowball. The Joker also increases your chances of drawing to a seven. Suppose you have this hand:

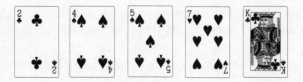

Obviously, any ace, three, six or Joker will make a seven hand, a total of thirteen cards. (Of course the ace or the Joker will make the best hand.)

However, if your hand was:

Any ace, three, five, or six will make the seven. Now you have sixteen cards that will make a good hand.

Poker is a game of small edges. The good player is always aware of the edges, no matter how small. Having the Joker in your hand is an edge. Therefore, it is elementary that if you have the Joker in your hand, you have the edge on the other players who do not have the Joker.

Lowball Strategies

Profitable strategies for lowball draw is a difficult subject to discuss in a precise manner. Knowing when to draw to an eight and which eight to draw to in any given situation is really the pivot point in becoming a solid player. Drawing to the seven is fairly routine and much simpler. Like any form of poker, knowledge of the other players is vital. There is a lot of bluffing in lowball. Knowledge about drawing to an eight and coping with a bluff does not come from a book. It comes from combat at the table.

There is one little ditty that typifies the play of a conservative or "rock" player:

> *Roses are red, violets are blue*
> *Don't draw to an eight and never draw two.*

That ditty falls into the category of a generalization. A professor of mine once reminded the class, "All generalizations are false, including this one." I will leave you with that, and the suggestion that you find some good literature specifically dealing with lowball poker.

2

STUD POKER

THE VERY FIRST HAND OF POKER I played was Seven-Card Stud, perhaps the most popular poker game in the world at that time. I don't recall if I won any matchsticks that night, but I did find out that I liked poker. In stud poker, some cards are exposed and other cards are dealt face down. Consequently, more information or clues are available to you and your opponents than draw poker. When you add to this the increased number of betting rounds in stud, you have the potential for good profit. It is my belief that all poker players should become knowledgeable in Seven-Card Stud. Five-Card Stud, although a good game, is not very popular in card rooms or casinos. However, trends come and go. At the time of this writing, Five-Card Stud's popularity is declining, perhaps due to the increasing popularity of the Hold 'Em games. But because Five-Card Stud is still played in home and apartment games, I will give you some basic playing information and elementary strategy.

FIVE-CARD STUD

This game is usually played with a 52-card deck (without the Joker) and often without an ante. If there is no ante, there is either a *blind* placed or a *forced bet*. The blind is usually the first player to the left of the dealer. If a forced bet is used, the player with the lowest card or the highest card is forced to make the first bet. I shall describe the process for a game with an ante.

After the ante is placed in the pot, each player is dealt one card face down and one card face up before there is a betting round. The first person to act can be either the person with the lowest card (which is believed to stimulate more action) or the highest card showing. This person can either check or bet.

The house rules vary on who is to initiate the action. If the house rules have the highest card start the betting and two or more aces are showing, the person with the first ace dealt is usually the one to act first. This rule of "first dealt" also applies when the low card is first to act. (Some games open by suits instead of "first dealt" when there are ties. Check for your local customs.)

When the betting round is completed, each active player receives another card face up. Then comes another betting round, and this time the highest hand on board is first to act. Then another card is delivered face up. After another betting round, the final card is dealt face up. Every active player at this point has four cards face up and one card face down. After the final betting round the hands are turned over and a winner is awarded the pot.

Five-Card Stud Strategy

The basic rule for a starting hand is to have the best hand. That means start either with a pair or with a hole card that is equal to or higher than any cards showing. If your hole card is equal to the highest card showing, your up card should be a ten or better.

The second most important rule is to fold if you are obviously beaten. For instance, if you have:

and catch a 7♠ on the next card but someone catches an ace, fold if someone bets.

How about this situation? What would you do? Suppose you have:

and you catch this card:

However, an opponent has this on the table (known as his *board)*:

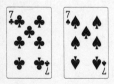

He bets. Should you fold?

Yes. Although you might run him down, remember he has almost as good a chance to improve his hand as you do. Sure you have three overcards and you might pair any of your three cards and win. However, while you are catching one pair, he might also be catching two pairs or even *trips* (three of a kind). (Or, he might have trips already!) To win in this situation, you *must* catch better than that opponent. In two out of three situations, your opponent has the edge. Save your money. Wait for the circumstance where you have the advantage. Be faithful to the rule, "When beaten in sight, get out."

Sometimes you will find yourself with an absolute lock on your opponent(s). Suppose you end up with this hand:

and your opponent has a board like:

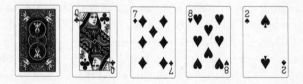

There is no possible way for you to lose. What you do now is often determined by house rules or customs. Some home games prohibit betting a lock. Some call this a courtesy of the game. Be sure to follow the local customs. My preference is to play the game as aggressively as I can. I believe getting a lock is exactly what I have been striving for, and so I bet as much as I think the customer will call. Unless I am playing in a game where the house rules or customs prohibit betting a lock, I will certainly bet the limit.

One other bit of advice: In general, don't try to draw for straights or flushes. They are terribly difficult to make in Five-Card Stud. Your moneymakers are top pairs, two pairs and trips.

SIX-CARD STUD

This is a game that has never become popular in public card rooms but is often played in home games. It is also played with the high/low adaptation.

Six-Card Stud is usually dealt one of two ways: First, somewhat like Five-Card Stud, the first card is dealt face down, four cards face up and the sixth card face down. This has the result of adding another round of betting. The second variation is to deal two cards face down and the last four face up. This version does not add a betting round.

Six-Card Stud Strategy

In Six-Card Stud, the average winning hand will be somewhat higher than Five-Card Stud. There is also a stronger possibility for straights and flushes. Therefore, starting hand requirements are proportionately higher. In early position, call only with hole card(s) equal to or higher than any showing and the up card a nine or better, or with a pair of eights or higher and no other matching card visible. In late position, call with high cards as above or with any pair when no matching cards showing. Fold hands like T♦-7♦-3♦ or 8♣-7♣-6♣. The drawing odds are too great, and you don't have strong possibilities of winning if you pair one or more of your cards.

As always in stud games, fold if beaten in sight. If you catch a pair of tens or better, raise to try to narrow the competition. If you catch two pairs on fourth street (see Glossary), bet as much as you can to narrow the field.

SEVEN-CARD STUD

There is no doubt in my mind that Seven-Card Stud will be around for a long time. Seven-Card Stud is a most demanding game, a game that requires a great card memory, great player evaluation and courage. Here is an example. Suppose an opponent had this porch:

Does that porch look dangerous? It looks like trash. There are no pairs showing, and yet it is possible for that opponent to have a jack-high straight, an ace-high straight, a spade flush, a whole slew of full houses, four sevens, four deuces, four jacks, four kings or a royal flush. If that does not make you respectful of Seven-Card Stud, there is nothing I can say that will. Seven-Card Stud is just one terrific challenge for the serious poker player.

The dealer deals two cards face down to each player and one card face up. The low card or the high card is the first to act. If the rules require a forced bet, at least a minimum bet is placed. If there is a tie for which card is the highest or lowest, either the first one dealt is required to act or else it goes alphabetically by suits (clubs, diamonds, hearts, spades). This betting round is called *third street.*

The fourth street card is also dealt face up and a betting round is declared. This time the highest hand showing is first to act. The fifth and sixth street cards are dealt face up, also followed by a betting round. The seventh street card is delivered face down, and the final betting round is held.

Seven-Card Stud Strategy

Because players get more cards than in five- or six-card stud games, try to build bigger, stronger hands. You do that with tough starting hand requirements, and certain draw hands become playable. Generally, raise with any pair of tens or bigger. One strong player calls these *premium* hands. Usually raise with them to try to eliminate some players. If you have good position and the pot is not raised, stay with small pairs unless you see a *trip card* (card needed to get three of a kind) exposed. In late position in unraised pots, stay with draw hands like:

or

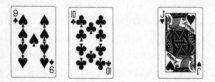

unless:

1. In the case of a flush draw, three cards or more of your suit are exposed.

2. In the case of a straight draw, three of the eights and/or queens are exposed.

Also count the sevens and kings. If three or more of them are exposed, fold.

If drawing for a flush and you do not catch your flush card on fourth street (the fourth round dealt face up by the dealer), fold unless the pot is huge and not more than three of your suit have appeared. Do the same with the straight draw. Generally, I advise the recreational player to improve on fourth street or give it up. Although there are situations that an experienced player will recognize that will permit profitable play if he or she does *not* improve on fourth street, I cannot recommend that for players who don't have a lot of experience. Of course, continue to observe the "beaten in sight" rule. It is seldom wise to go uphill unless you have other *good* drawing opportunities.

Card Memory—Card memory is extremely important in Seven-Card Stud. I suggest to my students that they start developing their card memory by looking first for cards that either help or hurt their own hands. If you have a pair dealt to you, check first to determine if either of your trip cards is showing. Then look for the cards that match your other card. If you have a hand like:

First check for any kings and then check for any tens that are showing.

If you have three cards of the same suit, count the exposed cards of your suit. For straight draws, count the cards needed to complete the straight. If you see four of your flush cards or three straight cards exposed, fold.

After you have investigated cards that will hurt your hands, look for cards that will impair the opponents' hands. If an opponent raises with a jack showing, check for other jacks. If a tight player calls with a king showing, count the kings. Since the ace is such a potent card, I also encourage students to keep track of all the aces. If someone folds an ace, keep the suit in mind. It might be quite useful later as you evaluate other hands. For instance, if you start with this hand:

and you catch the 8♣

and then catch the 3♣.

Since you have a second-high club draw and someone else has three hearts showing, you will be more comfortable if you have seen the ace of hearts folded. In that case, you will know that if you catch your club flush you have a very good chance of having the best flush.

If you are feeling overwhelmed by the necessity of card memory and the swiftness of the game, here is a tip. Try to sit in the first or second seat to the left of the dealer in casino and card room settings. This will give you a few more precious seconds to watch the cards as they are being dealt. Check your cards immediately and then watch the players and cards as they are being dealt. You have to be quick. But don't be discouraged. Practice is all it takes.

RAZZ OR SEVEN-CARD STUD LOW

If you like to gamble, you should play *Razz*. You will be joined by some wonderful folks who will throw a lot of money at the pot. Razz will challenge your heart muscles, strain your brain and put sweat in your palms. If you like to risk and bluff, Razz is your game.

The game is played exactly like Seven-Card Stud High except the highest card showing (excluding the ace, which is strictly a low card) on third street (the third round of cards dealt face up by the dealer) is usually a forced bet. The best low hand is the *wheel,* which is ace through five. Even though this is a straight, straights and flushes are ignored, just like California Lowball Draw. After the fourth street card has been dealt, the player with the lowest two cards is the first player to act. There are five betting rounds, and so there is usually a lot of money in the pot. If you learn to play this game well, you could win a lot of money.

Razz Strategy

The number one rule is, "The value of your hand is based on what cards other players are showing." If you have this hand:

and everyone else has a paint card *(face card)*, you have the best hand at that moment.

Or suppose you have this hand:

and there are two deuces, one four and two fives showing. If there is a raise, my advice would be to fold. Quite a number of the cards you need are showing and it is likely you do not have the best hand. Remember, the value of your hand is based on what cards other players have showing. Everyone can see that you have an eight and that will certainly make it rough. My suggestion for choosing your starting hands is again to be quite conservative until you get a lot of experience. The minimum starting hand to play against a strong board (the face-up cards of your opponents) is three cards, each of which is seven or below.

I personally am a bit reluctant to raise on third street even with a good hand. My reasoning is that I will fold more hands on fourth and fifth street than most of my opponents. I want the hand to develop a bit before I start pumping money into the pot. When I catch a good four-card low with a strong porch (my face-up cards), watch out!

SEVEN-CARD STUD, HIGH/LOW SPLIT

(8 or Better for Low)

This game is very popular. It has much of the appeal of straight high Seven-Card Stud and the added appeal to players who see the game as a way to at least get their money back. If a player has a lot of patience, and can avoid the traps, this is a very good game. The eight or better for low has increased the popularity of the game. That rule means you must have five unduplicated cards, all eight or lower, to win low. If no one has those five cards, eight or below, the high hand sweeps the pot.

Traps—There are some snares that will grab your money so fast you won't know what happened. This game takes some discipline. The biggest trap has already been mentioned. The escape hatch that many players hold on to is "trying to at least get their money back." When they play High/Low Split, they feel they can play more hands and bring home more money. Wrong!

Another major trap is players playing this game like they play Seven-Card Stud High. Wrong, wrong, wrong. For instance, a player dealt a pair of kings with a small card will often play and even raise. That is a very bad play.

Another trap is the violation of the "Fourth Street Paint" rule. Suppose you start with this hand:

That is a pretty good start. However, your next card is:

That jack is a paint, or undesirable face card. If there is a bet, you should fold. That is the paint rule. Even if you waited an hour for that starting hand, fold. It is discouraging to catch just one bad card that makes you fold, but sometimes it is necessary.

High/Low Split Strategy

The conventional strategy is to always think low. The only high hands to invest in are definite three-of-a-kind and a pair of aces, preferably with a low card. Seldom play a low hand that has an eight. The best starting hands are three low cards of one suit, preferably with the ace. Other good hands are any three wheel cards (ace-two-three, for example). These hands give you the opportunity to sweep high and low. Sweeps usually earn you three times as much money as a split.

3

HOLD 'EM POKER (FLOP GAMES)

THE NEWEST FAMILY OF POKER games that has become popular throughout the nation are the Hold 'Em games. Texas Hold 'Em is arguably the most popular game played in casinos and card rooms. Yet I find a lot of people who have never heard of Texas Hold 'Em. They know or have played Seven-Card Stud but have no idea how the flop games are played. If you are one of the people who are not familiar with Hold 'Em, you are in for a treat. These are some of the most exciting poker games ever invented.

The term "flop" comes from a distinguishing way of revealing the cards. The game is traditionally played with blinds rather than antes. There can be one, two or more blinds, depending on the house rules. Usually the blinds are placed to the left of the dealer. Sometimes the dealer also puts up a blind.

Live Straddle—Most Hold 'Em games permit a "live straddle." This is when the player to the left of the blinds puts up an optional blind bet. He also has the option of raising again when the action gets back to him. A live straddle is usually double the big blind. Suppose you are in a Texas Hold 'Em game with two blinds of $2 and $4. If allowed by the house rules, the live straddle would be $8. If a second live straddle was allowed, that would be $16. A live straddle is usually made by people who feel lucky or want to gamble. The disadvantage of a live straddle is that the player's position is poor. He will have to act before most of the other players. Depending on house rules, there can be several live straddles. When that happens, it is real gambling—because it is "live," which means the player can raise again when the action comes back to him.

How Hold 'Em Games Are Played

After a certain number of cards are dealt to each player, a betting round is held. At the completion of the betting round, the dealer "burns" a card (discards the top card) and places three cards face up in the center of the table. These are "community cards" and are commonly referred to as the *flop*. Everyone can use these cards in combination with his or her cards to make the best five cards they can. After another betting round, the dealer discards (burns) the top card and places one more card face up in the center. This card is usually called the *turn card*. Another betting round is held. The dealer burns a card and then places the last card (called the *river card*) face up in the center. After the fourth and last betting round, the hands are shown down and a winner is declared.

TEXAS HOLD 'EM

During the last part of April and first part of May, The World Series of Poker is held at Binion's Horseshoe Casino in Las Vegas, Nevada. That is a big event for poker players around the world. Every year players from every state and many foreign countries gather to play poker. While there are tournament events scheduled for each of the most popular poker games, the main event is Texas Hold 'Em. The main event is a $10,000 buy-in, no-limit tournament. Basically, you put down $10,000 for a seat and chips. The winner the last few years has taken home at least $1,000,000. My point in this paragraph is not the one million dollars, but that the game chosen for this huge event is Texas Hold 'Em. That demonstrates the challenge and the attractiveness of the game. In my opinion, Texas Hold 'Em is the prince of poker games, the game that demands the most skill and courage.

To my knowledge this is the only worldwide championship event where anyone can participate and have a reasonable chance of beating the world-class players. Can you imagine entering the ring against a boxing world champion? Or playing tennis against a Wimbledon champion? Several amateurs have won the big prize in the World Series of Poker.

The different Hold 'Em games are distinguished by the number of cards dealt to each player to start the game. In Texas Hold 'Em, only two cards are dealt to each player. In Omaha Hold 'Em, four cards are dealt to each player. In Pineapple Hold 'Em, three cards are dealt. In all the different adaptations and mutations of these three basic games, the flop remains consistent. Three cards on the flop, one card on the turn and one card on the river or fifth street. Like other poker games, only five cards are used to determine the winner. The sixth, seventh, and all other cards are not used to calculate the winner. Only the best five cards. If there is a tie in the five cards, the pot is divided. There is never a time when a sixth card is used to break a tie.

Texas Hold 'Em Strategy

Position is extremely important in all the Hold 'Em games. I will be referring to early, middle and late positions. In a ten-handed game, when I refer to early position I am referring to the three players to the left of the dealer or dealer button. The next four players are considered in the middle position and the last three players are in late position. Be aware that other authors may have their own definitions of early, middle and late positions.

Position and starting hands are closely interrelated. In an early position, when the dealer button is close to you on your right, you should only play VERY big cards. Preferably, the playable hands are the three big pairs, ace-king suited and ace-queen suited. If you are learning the game, be very careful in playing in early positions. Most players, including some experienced, good Hold 'Em players, lose money in the early positions.

Middle positions provide for more flexibility. You can play all the hands listed above, preferably raising with them, and you can profitably play ace-jack suited, the middle pairs (jacks, tens, nines and eights) and king-queen suited. I suggest you not play queen-jack or jack-ten suited from middle position until you become more skilled. Experience will teach you to recognize opportunities and dangers. Knowing when to dump a hand is very important.

It is in late position that the game of Texas Hold 'Em becomes fun. Good players wait patiently through the early and middle positions and become creative in the back. The choice of starting hands increases dramatically in late position. More hands become profitable. Occasionally, I will even raise with such trash as queen-ten off-suit if the pot has not been raised and I sense weakness in the other players. Do you see why I say that position and starting hands are interrelated? The hands you should never even play up front become raising hands in back. The value of the hand in itself does not change, but the power of position has a dramatic impact on how and what you can play and show a profit. This concept is incredibly important for a Texas Hold 'Em player.

Reading the Flop—Because of the community card feature, some novice players have trouble reading the flop. Be aware that there *must* be three cards of one suit among the community cards for a flush to be possible. Sometimes four or even five cards of one suit appear on the board.

Suppose you have played this hand:

The flop looks like this after all the cards are out:

Every active player now has a spade flush. You have the *second nut* (second best possible) hand with the king of spades. If someone else has the ace of spades, he or she wins. If no one has a spade in their hand, the dealer will divide the money between the active players. When the highest possible hand is on the board, the pot is split. This is what is known as "the board plays." One important word of caution. You must turn your cards over so the dealer can see them to get a share of the pot. I have seen it happen many times that a player will not recognize that the board plays and will simply throw his hand away. That makes it impossible for the dealer to give that person his share of the pot. Whenever in doubt, turn your cards face up and let the dealer read the hand.

In Texas Hold 'Em you can play both cards from your hand, one card from your hand or even no cards from your hand. Here is an example of the best possible five cards being on the board. If this were the board, who would win?

The answer is that every active player would play the board. No one could possibly beat the quad deuces with an ace. However, if the board finished like this, who would win?

The correct answer and the winner of the money would be the person with the highest single card in his hand that is higher than the ten. If one person had a jack, another a king and a third a queen, the person with the king would win.

Learning to read the flop is one of the first lessons for anyone learning to play Texas Hold 'Em. I recommend some additional homework. I suggest you take a deck of cards and flop three cards, determine what is the nut hand, deal another card (turn card) and determine if the nuts have changed; and then take the final card (river card) and do the same thing. Just a little practice is all it takes.

OMAHA HOLD 'EM

Omaha Hold 'Em is played basically like Texas Hold 'Em, except that each player is dealt four cards face down. These four cards, combined with the five that will eventually be the community cards, make Omaha Hold 'Em a nine-card poker game

(Texas Hold 'Em is a seven-card game). I'm sure you have already guessed that a nine-card poker game will have some huge hands. In fact, those extra two cards dramatically change the complexion of the game. I generally refer to Omaha as a card game and Texas Hold 'Em as a people game. In Omaha Hold 'Em, quite often you just try to build the absolute nut hand and not worry nearly as much about what the other players are doing.

There is one extremely important change of rules from Texas Hold 'Em to Omaha Hold 'Em. In Omaha Hold 'Em you *must* play two cards from your hand. Two and only two. Never one, never three or four. This rule is often costly for the novice. You will remember that in Texas Hold 'Em, you could play one, two or none of your cards to combine with the community cards to form the best five cards. *Not so in Omaha Hold 'Em.* Again, you must play two cards from your hand—no more, no less.

For example, suppose you have this hand:

After all the cards are out on the board it looks like this:

Do you have a flush? Not in Omaha. In Texas Hold 'Em, you would have the best possible cards, or nuts. In Omaha, you would have two pairs, kings and queens. Does that illustrate the difference? Keep in mind the rule is to play two cards from your hand and three from the board.

Check out this. Do you have a full house? This is your hand:

The flop is:

A lot of newcomers to Omaha will think they have a full house, eights full of aces. All you have is three of a kind. Remember, two from hand, three from board!

Choosing a good starting hand is probably the toughest job any player has in Omaha. There are any number of reasons to play each and every hand. Some players will play 80 to 90 percent of all hands dealt to them. Let's look at both the high version and the high/low split variant and try to define what consists of a good starting hand.

Omaha Hold 'Em High Strategy

One important fact emerges immediately. A good Omaha hand is not the combination of two Texas Hold 'Em hands. Why not? Because a good Omaha hand is a total of six two-card combinations. The first thing you look for when you pick up your four cards is how those cards work together and interface. Premium hands are made up of high cards that coordinate. Here is an example:

This hand has a big pair of kings; the nut club hand if clubs are dealt; the second nut spade flush possibility; and three parts of *Broadway* (an Ace-high straight).

Premium hands create few problems in choosing to play them or not. They can be played from any position and can call a raise. But what about this hand?

Can you call with that hand? You have that same pair of kings, but those other two cards are almost worthless. Muck (fold) that hand, unless you are in last position in a pot that has not been raised.

What about this hand?

Can you call? Absolutely not. This is the typical hand made up of two playable Texas Hold 'Em hands. However, there is no integration beyond the Q-K and 6-7. The other combinations are poor; K-6, K-7, Q-6, Q-7. Four of the six combinations do not work together.

Another problem with most Omaha hands is that they are three-legged; they will have three really good cards and one stranger. Unless you can play them cheap from late position, fold them.

One more problem is that neither of the above hands have the best possible flush draw. Look at that hand with the pair of kings above. That could cost you a bundle if three spades were flopped in the community cards and you called all the way only to lose to the ace-high spades. It happens a lot! Having the second best possible hand at a particular point in the game is tempting but costly. The hand appears too good to throw away, but one is afraid to bet or raise with it. Beware of this "second nut" trap.

Omaha Hold 'Em is essentially a game of drawing for the best possible hand at each point in the game (the nuts). Stick with that philosophy until you know the game.

OMAHA HOLD 'EM, HIGH/LOW SPLIT

(8 or Better for Low)

This variety of Omaha has become quite popular. It offers plenty of action, and you can find reasons to play almost any hand if you try hard enough. If you have enough money, you certainly can play almost every hand. My problem is that I like to win. Therefore I am extremely careful in choosing my starting hands.

High/Low Split Omaha Strategy

Again, starting hand selection is an important key for turning a profit from this poker enterprise. The integration of the four cards is vital. For this High/Low game, the low side becomes extremely important. Therefore, a solid hand contains good low draw possibilities. I believe that a hand that does not have an ace is almost unplayable. Obviously, if you watch an Omaha Hold 'Em game and see seven or eight people call the bets, a lot of the players do not have an ace. That is the beauty of Omaha. Lots of players contesting for the pot with only a few knowing what hands take down the money.

The keys to showing a profit are choosing the right hand to start and lots of patience. You will find some big swings in terms of your chips. It seems that dry spells come along quite often, punctuated occasionally with a winning streak. When you catch a few winners in a row, your stacks go up like crazy because of the size of the pots. Walk a careful line at this point. Push your hot streak but also don't go too far. Always be aware that Omaha is a game where you play the nuts. If you don't have the nuts, you will lose—big. I almost always adhere to the axiom, "Have the best hand or the best draw or get out." The incredible part is that the other players keep paying you off if they have second, third and even fourth nut. Some of my strategies for playing Omaha:

1. Bet the hell out of the nuts.
2. Only call on the nut draw hands.
3. Never *slow-play* (this means to let other players take the lead in betting), except for quads.
4. Beware of the *underfull* hand (a full house that is not the highest possible one).

PINEAPPLE HOLD 'EM

There is a crazy game that needs to be mentioned at least in passing. Pineapple Hold 'Em is a sort of hybrid between Texas Hold 'Em and Omaha Hold 'Em. You are dealt three cards face down instead of two or four. At some point you must discard one of these cards, either before the flop or after, depending on the house rules. Like Texas Hold 'Em, you can play one, none or both of the cards in your hand. Where I live, the discard before the flop is called *stripper*. Pineapple Hold 'Em is played straight high or high/low. I call it an insane action game because it has such funny variations and is really tough to figure out. When I am trapped into playing it, my rules are to draw only at the nut flush; and to have trips or better on the flop and/or the nut low draw if the game is high/low. If your bent is for some wild and bizarre action, try Pineapple Hold 'Em. Be sure to find out all the local rules because those rules vary a lot from place to place.

SECTION II

STRATEGY

The game of poker is deceptive. It looks so simple, and in truth, just about anyone can learn the basics in a short while. I compare learning poker to the time I took my first course in college psychology. I was fascinated by psych. The more I learned, the more I discovered there was to learn. However, there was a turning point where I could formulate categories and compartmentalize the information into digestible bite-size portions. Once I got to that point, psych was a joy. The same can be said for poker. I predict there will be a point very soon where you will be able to compartmentalize this poker information and digest it quickly. Most important, you will be applying this information at the table. Then poker becomes a joy.

Primarily there are four strategic principles that form the cornerstones of solid poker play. I call these cornerstones Patience, Position, Planning and Emotional Control. They are essential ingredients for successful poker play, and it is important that you study them carefully. I have also included some information in this section on basic math, general preparation for the actual combat situations you will encounter in poker, and a few of the old axioms of poker that are as true today as they were fifty or a hundred years ago. Remember, these are very basic instructions. Read this material over and over until you grasp what I am saying. Then play a little and try to apply these directions. Expect to climb the mountain of knowledge slowly. Poker is a complex game, and what I am writing about in this section is vital to successful and profitable play.

STRUCTURED BETTING VERSUS SPREAD LIMITS

As part of your preparation you should be aware of the major divisions in the betting stipulations. These divisions usually do not apply for home games but "structured" limits versus "spread" limits are important to know when and if you play in casinos or card rooms. Home games are usually spread limits and if they aren't, the new people are told as soon as the game begins.

Structured Betting

Before we get into strategy, I need to back up a bit and describe the two different ways the betting is carried out in a poker game. At the time of this writing most casino and card clubs have structured betting. Let me illustrate with a $3–$6 game. The structure means that you can bet exactly $3 (no more, no less) for the first two betting rounds and exactly $6 in each betting round thereafter. All bets and all raises must be in these increments. The key to identifying a structured game is the hyphen between the numbers. (Sometimes a slash [/] is used.)

A spread limit is a different form of betting. In spread limit you can bet any amount between the limits. In the case of a spread limit game of say $1 to $5 you are permitted to bet $1, $2, $3, $4 or $5 at any time. The key to identifying the differences between structure and spread limits is the spread limit would be written with a "to" between the numbers; $1 to $6. The structured game would have the hyphen. See the difference?

Let me illustrate a $3–$6 structured game with the five betting intervals in Seven-Card Stud.

> The three cards are dealt to each player, two down, one up. At this point there is a betting interval. All bets would be the lower number, in this case, $3. The next card is dealt face-up. This is called fourth street. Again a betting interval of $3. The next card is dealt face-up. This is called fifth street. This time the only amount you can bet (or raise) is $6. The next card is dealt face-up, called, you guessed it, sixth street. Again the betting interval is $6. The last card is dealt facedown and all betting is at the $6 level.

Spread Limits

If the game is described with a "to" between the numbers, then it is the spread limit variety. In a $1 to $5 game you can bet any amount between $1 and $5 at each betting interval. Raises are slightly different. Let's suppose the first person bet $1. The next person could either call the $1 or raise any amount from $1 to $5. If the first person bet $3, the next person could either call the $3 or raise it the amount of the bet ($3) or any greater number, in this case $3, $4 or $5. Any raises must be at least the size of the original bet or greater. This might seem a bit complicated at first, but it makes sense after you play a few moments.

There is another variety of the spread limit game you should know about. It is a game like $1 to $5, with $10 after the last card is dealt. This is just exactly like the other spread limit game with the extra possibility of betting $10 after all the cards have been dealt to the players. All bets can now be any number between $1 and $10. This just adds some spice to the game and some players love it and others don't like it at all.

Remember, listen or look for the key—the "to" between the numbers—that indicates a spread limit. If the "to" isn't there, the game is probably a structured game.

4

PATIENCE

BECAUSE WE ALL HAVE THAT powerful desire to compete, we need tricks and techniques to help us quell that craving. I have found it is usually easy to control the urge to play during the first hour or so at the table. Gradually, this resolve slips away. It becomes increasingly tempting to fudge on starting hands, stay one or two cards too long and allow "hope" to influence our calls. If you can be patient enough to wait for the right starting hand and allow it to develop correctly, you will have a distinct advantage over the other players.

An experienced poker player can immediately tell who the most patient players are in a poker game after only watching one or two rounds. He simply watches who throws away the most hands. If this same experienced poker player sees 80% to 90% of the players participating in each hand, he has found what he is looking for—a loose game with unseasoned, impatient players anxious to win big. He sees a field of grain ready for the harvest, some cattle ready for the market. He buys his chips and sits down, ready to reap.

THE BENEFITS OF PATIENCE

The experienced poker player knows that only a few hands dealt out have a high winning percentage potential. So he waits *pa-*

tiently for those hands. He does not try to play out a trash hand hoping it will win. Chances are it won't.

A patient poker player knows that the cards will come to him eventually. That is a proven fact. So when one good hand gets "run down" or beaten by some stupid play, the patient player knows the good cards will come again, and if he or she has a tolerant attitude, the patient player will take home the money. That patient player simply relaxes and waits until he gets another quality starting hand and plays that as well as he is able.

The experienced poker player will play very few marginal hands, and he will play them only under certain favorable circumstances. He will carefully measure in his mind the cost of investment against the possible gain, if lady luck should smile upon him.

Starting hands are one important part of patience and the poker player. You want to start with the best hand or have the best draw. The theory is that when you have the lead, the others have to run faster to catch you. They have to be luckier than you are to win. They are going uphill, not you. Put the burden on them, not on your own back. So you wait until you get the right hand in the right position. Then you play. Not before.

This is much easier said than done, because as poker players, we love to compete. Hence, it is easy to stay with a mediocre hand to the bitter end, hoping for an extraordinary stroke of luck.

But the odds are against you. Suppose you are playing in a Seven-Card Stud game with six other players. If lady luck dealt her favors exactly even, how many hands each round would you win? One out of seven hands! Then why in the world would you play the other six hands? Why give your money away in situations where you are not the favorite to win?

This is admittedly a bit of an exaggeration, and some people would say that you can't know who is going to win unless you play. However, the smart player will play only those hands that give him a good to great opportunity to take down the pot.

Patience After the Opening Bell

Imagine this scene: You have thrown away the last 37 hands in a Texas Hold 'Em game. Now you have great position, four people have called the blind bet and you look down at your hand and you see two jacks. Two jacks are a better than average hand, but it is also a dangerous hand. It appears stronger than it is.

Your heart beats a bit faster. You raise the pot and four people call your raise. Now you have a very nice pot. Those chips would sure look good on your stack. The flop comes:

Your heart sinks. The first player bets and two other players call. What should you do? The answer should be very obvious. If you are not already beaten, you certainly will be if another diamond should come. Or a ten or a king or even another jack could make you a second or third best hand. You don't have the jack of diamonds either, so you really have no alternative but to throw those jacks in the muck pile. A patient player would do this without giving it another thought. Throw those losers away without investing another cent or matchstick.

Just because you had a great start at the first couple of cards does not mean that you should play out the hand to the end.

When the following cards fall in such a way that it makes your hand the underdog, get rid of it. Exercise your patience. Here is the same concept in Seven-Card Stud. You start with a buried pair of tens with a nine showing. You are in middle position so you raise. A lady with a king showing calls you. The next card you get is a jack. The lady catches another king. She glances over at you and then bets. What should you do? Again, don't even think about it. Throw those losers away. She has you beaten at the moment, and she might even have a third king in the hole. You started with a good hand, but it went to pieces on the next card. Get out while you can without losing any more money.

My recommendation is to be extremely tight the first hour of play. I mean extremely tight. Get a feel for the game, for the players. Who is playing loose. Who likes to raise with a draw hand (see Glossary). Who will bet from the last position with nothing. Who will call all bets, regardless of what he has. Who is on tilt. Who is running strong. Who is getting good hands beaten and is moaning and groaning. Play only very, very solid starting hands from any position. If you play a hand and get only a little improvement on the next card or cards, get out and watch the action. When you feel you are somewhat familiar with the players and the type of action that is happening, loosen up just a tad.

If you do as I recommend, I promise you will be happier and richer. You will see things you didn't understand before. You will notice new things about players you thought you knew quite well. I also predict you will establish a table image that will work well for you. The other players will notice you are only playing a few hands and respect your raises. When that starts to happen, you change your style and do some fancy stuff from late position. When you are called and you show down a hand, they will be astounded and confused. That confusion is exactly what you want.

Don't Be What You See

Copying the play of other people is a trap you should avoid at all costs. You will see someone play the most terrible cards and bet into dangerous situations and still win. His or her chips will pile up and you will ask yourself if maybe you should play like that. Don't do it. Be patient. Soon you will notice that the person who played wild and crazy is now losing and is getting down to the bottom of his big pile of chips. The laws of probability will eventually catch up with the loose and impatient poker player.

I was watching a lady play Seven-Card Stud one night. She called a raise with a pair of sevens, and one of the sevens that would make her three-of-a-kind (trips) was showing in another person's hand. It was a terrible call. Needless to say, she caught the *case card* (the last card of a particular rank left in the deck) and won the hand. Her three sevens beat two pairs, kings over queens. She drew out on the guy who had her beaten until the last card. If you see that kind of play and emulate it, you will be one of the huge percentage of poker players that are losers.

Early on, when I was learning Texas Hold 'Em, I raised with a pair of aces. Someone called my raise with the K♦-5♥. The flop came:

My opponent had flopped the bottom pair. He was a huge underdog to my pair of aces. However, he called my bet. He also called my bet after the turn card, the 3♣. The river card was 5♦. He raised me after I bet, and he won the pot with three fives. He had drawn out on me with a very longshot draw. Nonetheless, I was most impressionable in those early days. I saw him win the pot with a bottom pair and decided that must be how you should play this game. Oh, how wrong I was. I had copied some bad play, and that cost me a lot of money before I caught on to the percentages.

You will see a lot of that bad play in almost all low-limit poker games. People love to play, and very few are willing to bother to study the game to determine what is good play and what is bad play. My advice: Don't be what you see.

Exceptions—There is a very obvious exception to this. Try to become aware of who at your table can really play. Watch closely who consistently wins the chips. Also, a very big clue to competency at the poker table is to watch how many hands per round a suspected good player plays. Often the tipoff to a good player is the few pots he or she enters. Then also observe whatever hands he or she turns over. At that point you can replay the hand in your head and it will tell you what they did at each point of action. Did they have good position to call or raise with that particular hand? Did they have a solid reason to call a raise? Did they have the best hand or the best draw? Once you get a solid indication that a certain player is good, then you can learn from him or her. From then on, watch them closely to learn how they chose to play in any particular circumstance. Then examine that strategy and decide if it will work for you.

As a general rule, be quite skeptical of how others play. They will lead you wrong more often than not. Be on the lookout for a good player to model your betting strategy after, but do so only after you examine his play to see if it is dependable. Avoid the mistake that I made.

MAKE THE CARDS YOUR SERVANTS

"Ha," you say, "Old Andy has lost it. His neurons are not connecting with the brain cells. He writes, 'Make the cards your servants?' That is crazy. No one can make the cards obey their wishes." I agree, but hear me out. Maybe there is some truth here. Some players let the cards control their actions. For instance, they see a pair, any pair, in Seven-Card Stud. They automatically call. They don't consider the possible ramifications of that call. Say they catch a pair of sevens. They don't notice one of their sevens is showing. If they had checked around the board, they would have seen another seven being folded by Harriet. That is one big reason not to call with that pair of sevens. Also, Casey is a wild rammer-jammer and he has an ace showing. You can almost bet that Casey will raise the pot, even if has nothing to go with that ace. That is just the way he plays. However, you can never be sure what Casey has. He is just a rash and reckless player and is great to have in the game. That is another good reason to not call with that pair of sevens. When Casey is in the hand, you want to have a solid hand with good possibilities. That pair of sevens, with one other seven already gone, is not a solid hand. When you play a hand with Casey, you know you will be investing quite a bit of money. You only want to invest that kind of money in a hand that has good possibilities to win. The patient player will throw away any hand that does not present good to great possibilities.

Folding that pair of sevens is how you make the cards your servants. If you play every pair that comes along regardless of the circumstances, you will not be a successful player. The cards will have control. Patience will allow you to be in control.

Make those cards meet certain standards before you will play them. If you allow the rhythm of the cards to play you instead of you playing at the rhythm you wish, the cards are your masters. If a fair hand in a dangerous situation moves you to call, you are being controlled. Master the cards, or they will master you. Making automatic calls with any hand is not good.

A LIFELONG TASK

Players who really want to succeed at poker take the long view. They become dedicated to the craft of winning at this game. They

work at research, at reading players, at looking for good circumstances, at emotional control. They view the game of poker as
having the potential to make them money all of their lives. Therefore they dedicate some energy toward really learning how to play.
They are competitors in the true sense. They develop courage to
bet their hands, they discipline themselves to become stoic, they
are patient, they develop good friendships with comrades and they
develop an integrity within themselves. They are honest to the
core. If they borrow money, they are conscientious in paying it
back on time. The true poker players have competed in the arena
of life and the green felt. They deserve respect.

5

POSITION

THE CORRECT UNDERSTANDING and employment of position will do two things for you. One, it will make you money. Two, it will save you money. It is my feeling that the second, saving money, is even more important than the first.

The power of position comes from the information one receives when the other players act first. Few concepts have greater impact on playing poker than position. Some good authors have stated they do not feel a player can win consistently without a solid understanding and utilization of position. I agree with those authors.

The information you collect when you are last to act can turn a losing session into a winning session. Rephrased into one sentence, "Playing position correctly simply means more profit for you." With that message firmly in mind, let's expand on some ways to play position correctly.

RANDOM POSITION GAMES

I make the distinction between random position games and fixed position games. Random position games are games like Seven-

Card Stud where the first person to act is dependent upon the cards that appear. Some games require the high card start the action; others require that the lowest card (ace excluded) be first to act. After the initial betting round, the highest hand on board or the lowest hand on board must act first. If you are playing straight high Seven-Card Stud, the highest hand must check or bet first. If you are playing Seven-Card Stud Low (also named Razz), the lowest two cards must check or bet first. If you are playing Seven-Card Stud High/Low Split, the house rules most often require the highest hand on board to start the action. Almost all stud games are random position games.

Playing correct position in a random position game takes a bit more care and practice than in a fixed position game. For instance, say you call the opening bet in a Seven-Card Stud game with a ten showing. The person who made the first bet had a king as his up card. That person was next to you on the left. That meant you were last to act. When the next round of cards was distributed, the person on your right got an ace, which made him the first to act. If he bets, you are then under the gun and must call his bet, raise or fold. You have no opportunity to see what the other players will do. Since you caught a jack to pair one of your hole cards, you decide to call. The next card brings you a ten and gives you a pair showing on the table, making you the high hand and first to act. In three rounds you have gone from last to second to first in three cards. This fluctuation of betting position is not at all uncommon.

The point I am trying to make is in a random position game, you must be constantly reviewing your decisions based on a fluctuating position. A hand that was an okay call in late position is suddenly vaulted as first to act. You must examine the consequences of that position and its vulnerability. You must also examine quickly the lucrative possibilities that can occur. For instance, you could hold this hand on fourth street:

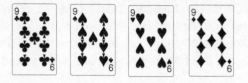

That is close to an unbeatable hand. What should be done? How should you bet that powerhouse in order to maximize the return?

If the pair of nines showing is first to act, you might want to check and hope some players catch up a bit. Giving a free card here will not hurt your chances of winning. Also, checking that pair of nines will confuse your opponents. You could also check-raise. Some players might bet this hand of quad nines and hope to get raised. My inclination would be to wait until after the fifth street card when the limits double in a structured game. Then I would check-raise, if I thought another person would bet. From that point on, I would lead bet if I were first to act. The choice of your actions must be made quickly and much will depend on what the other players have and how they are playing their hands. If everyone is being very, very cautious, it might be best to lead bet and hope for the best. If the action is wild and crazy, you can lay back and let the others carry the action for the time being. Another factor to consider is the table image that you have. If the other players consider you a *rock*, they might not call even one bet from you.

FIXED POSITION GAMES

Some of the most popular games employ a dealer button to indicate which player is either the dealer or the designated dealer. These games include most draw games and all the flop games. Position is fixed for any given hand. The same person is the first person to act on each and every betting round as long as that person is active in the hand. If the first person should fold, the action moves to the next person on the left. Because each player knows in advance what his or her position will be for that hand, the choice of starting hands and continuing play is somewhat easier.

PLAYING FROM BAD POSITION

When I get into trouble, it is usually because I play a hand out of position. Most recreational players are not aware of how costly it can be to get involved in a hand when out of position. Since I am beyond the recreational player stage, I should never be guilty of this expensive transgression, right? Well, I truly wish that were so. Every once in a while I yield to the temptation to play a jack-ten off-suit in early middle position in a Texas Hold 'Em game. My hand might look like this:

I am hoping that no one will raise the pot, but sure enough, the button or dealer raises. Now I am faced with a dilemma. Should I throw my hand away? Should I call the raise? There will probably be a total of four players who will call the raise if I do. I go ahead and call because the pot odds are good. The flop comes:

This whole hand is turning into a nightmare. I have flopped the second pair (the two jacks), but my kicker, the ten, is not good. There are also several draws, straight draws and a club draw. Then consider the guy who raised. Did he make a position raise or does he have a real hand? Maybe he has the king-queen. Maybe ace-king. Maybe a pair of tens. What to do? I wish I had never stayed in this hand. This could cost me a bundle if I challenge him. Should I lead bet? Should I check and call all the rest of the way, hoping to improve? I hate being a wimp like that, but I don't want to be stupid either. I might have the best hand, but it will cost some money to find out. There is now quite a bit of money in the pot, and there is promise of a great deal more. Is it worth the risk?

Remember where my position is? All the players on my right have folded. Everyone involved in the hand will act after I do. If I bet, one or more of them could raise and I couldn't call the raise and so I lose my bet. I could check with the best hand and give them all a free card. This position is horrible. I would be much better off if I had not played the hand at all. Think about this scenario. If you are not careful, it could happen to you a lot.

PLAYING FROM GOOD POSITION

The above was an example of how you may be tempted to play a marginal hand from bad position and how that act can cost you money. Now let's look at an example of how correct position can make you money. Let's use that very same hand:

This time the hand is dealt to you in last position in that Texas Hold 'Em game. You call the unraised blind bet. Again, the flop looks like this:

Everyone checks and you are the last to act. You can reasonably assume that if someone had an ace, they would have placed a bet, so you throw in a bet to see what will happen. One person calls. The next card is:

The other guy checks, you bet and win the pot.

This is an example of how position can win you money. Same hand played, J♦-T♣, with the same flop. The only difference was in position.

THE POWER OF POSITION

That was just a very simple illustration of the power of position. For the recreational player, it might seem like a lot to comprehend at first. As you study the game and look for these opportunities, you will become aware of just how powerful position is. There have been many sessions where I ended up with a small to moderate win because I was able to capitalize on position play. I was able to pick up small pots by recognizing that no one had anything. I didn't have anything either, but by betting from late or last position, I was able to win the pot.

Aggressive Play

What I like to do is look for situations where I can be the aggressor. For instance, in the above illustration where the J♦-T♣ was dealt in early middle position, it would be foolish to be aggressive. You don't have the card strength to take a strong stance. Where the J♦-T♣ was dealt on the button, I would sometimes even throw in a raise before the flop of the community cards. I would do so more often if there were some timid players at the table. I want them to look at me, to be afraid of me. A raise tends to intimidate. After the flop, most of the time players will check to the raiser. In this case, I have flopped the second pair with a poor to moderate kicker. However, I have the advantage of position. I make full use of that power. When they check to me, I will bet to clarify the hand. If I get check-raised, I throw my hand away. If a club comes on the next card, I check. If I catch another jack, I bet. If I catch a ten (giving me two pairs), I bet. If a nothing card comes, I bet. After the last card is dealt, if I have not improved, I will check. The pot is big enough for the quality of my hand. If someone has slow-played (to let others take the lead in betting) an ace, he will certainly call a last bet. Also, if someone else has improved and is waiting to check-raise, I will short-circuit his play. Now I don't win all the time with this strategy, but I win a lot more than I lose by being aggressive. When I have the power of position going for me, I become more aggressive.

Position vs. the Best Hand

I usually get an argument from one or more students when I discuss position in my classes. The student will say that the best hand is the best hand, and it will win regardless of position. Absolutely. I have no quarrel with that. IF you have the best hand you can play fast and loose. Maybe it would be more accurate to say that if you *knew* you had the best hand, you could play fast and loose. I find, however, that most of the time, you will not know when you have everyone beaten. It usually is quite chancy. In the example above, I might have had the best hand or I could have been dead last. In low-limit games, it is often extremely difficult to read the other players. Some players will slow-play huge hands and lead you to believe you are the leader. Some players will never raise regardless of what they have. How then can you put them on a hand or figure out what cards they hold? They just call and call and call. You could have a pair of kings and they could have a pair of aces and you would not suspect it. What a surprise when you turn the cards over. You had expected to win and didn't. I have seen players get really angry because of that kind of timid play. In situations like that, I agree that position means nothing. The best hand will win.

Information

The greatest power that position gives you is information. You will be able to observe how the other players act on their hands. If you sense weakness, which is often the case, you have a clear advantage. If you sense strength, and you have a moderate hand, throw it away.

When other players act before you, you know more than they do. It is quite simple. They send you messages on the strength of their hands based on how they bet, check, call or raise. This allows you to act in an appropriate and profitable way. If they are betting strongly and you have a weak hand, get out. If they are weak and you are strong, bet them out of the game. If they are weak and you are weak, you have the power of position, and you can take the pot.

Position is *always* a consideration, in every hand and every situation. Even a trash hand has value added to it if you catch it in excellent position. I have won a lot of money with trash hands from late position in Texas Hold 'Em. Once I called with a 5♣-3♠ in last position and flopped two pairs. Not only did I win a nice pot, but I got a lot mileage out of the reputation of playing a trash hand. All the players had put me in the rock (conservative) category, so they were shocked and confused by that risky, aggressive play. From then on, I only played quality cards and got called a lot by people who were confused as to what I might be playing.

6

PLANNING

PLANNING IS THE THIRD cornerstone of a good poker foundation. Planning is the head work, the energy put into thinking about the game. I know most recreational players play poker to recreate. (Clever conclusion, don't you think?) They play poker to relax. They want to step back from their regular stressful lives and have a little fun. They want to drink a little, talk smart and have a good time. To think about the game, "to plan," takes a lot of work, application and focus. My suggestion that these players do some planning might be just the opposite of what they want to do.

However, I like to win. My grandfather said, "Winning beats losing." Therefore this book is dedicated to giving Lady Luck a better shot at helping us win. When she has to do all the work, she gets in a bit of a snit at times. She likes our assistance. And she rewards us. As the salesman said, "The harder I work, the luckier I get." The more support we give to the Lady of Luck, the more substantial our bankroll becomes. Success in almost any enterprise is directly related to the perspiration level we expend. Poker is not like bingo. There is no skill in bingo. Bingo is just a plain old-fashioned brainless activity. To become a successful poker player, you need to think. In order to win, you need to engage the brain cells and examine opportunities and options.

For instance, you need to plan to be patient. You need to focus on what hands you can play. You need to plan to wait for the right hand in the right circumstance.

You need to plan to use position correctly. You need to think about how to take advantage of the power of position. Are you getting what I'm trying to say?

In the next chapter I will deal with emotional control. You especially need a scheme to employ emotional control. In poker, you have got to let the head lead, not the emotions. If the emotions lead, you are in deep trouble. Planning is a part of that head work. Planning is a cornerstone for making money at poker. Planning is also intimately connected with the other three cornerstones.

PLANNING FOR BETTING OPTIONS

Let me give you some examples on how to plan for betting strategies if the cards fall your way. For example, let's assume you are in a low-limit Seven-Card Stud game. Now, what do you do when you are dealt a pair of kings in the hole and an eight is showing? What is your plan?

You are third to act. What plan or betting strategy will win you the most money? If you have thought about this ahead of time, you don't have to waste valuable milliseconds contemplating, and you will be able to have more time to scan the up cards and the faces and/or reactions of other players. The most logical and profitable betting strategy here is to raise the limit with that pair of kings or any big pairs. With a pair of kings, you want to narrow the field and eliminate the competition as soon as possible. A pair of kings is a good hand, but it usually needs to improve to win. Also you want to find out if there is a better hand out against you. If a player with an ace showing calls or raises, you could be in trouble. Get this warning as quickly as you can. If you catch a whiff of trouble or an alarm bell sounds, slow it down.

As another example in the Seven-Card Stud game, you start with this hand:

The next card is:

You now have two pairs. How are you going to play this? What is your plan? You have seen no other tens or fours. Should you raise? Call? Call a raise? Re-raise? If you have thought about it, you have an advantage. If you have a blueprint, you can act with more authority.

What would I do? I would never call. I would either raise, re-raise or fold. I want to narrow the field, get out the three-card flush draws, some straight draws and those clowns who draw for a draw. I figure I probably have the best hand (with those two pairs) at the moment, but it doesn't have a great chance (23%) to improve to a full house. I would certainly bet it hard in a structured betting game. The limits double on fifth street in a structured game. I will bet and/or raise on fourth street, but because of the increased bets on fifth street, I will slow down. At this point, I don't want to invest any more money in this hand unless I can improve or be convinced that my opponent(s) are still drawing. While I am probably the leader on fourth street, these two pairs, tens and fours, will likely lose money unless I can run people off the pot. When the limits double on fifth street, I will check and call. Therefore I would probably check the hand on both fifth and sixth street. (Many authors have written about the affliction of two pairs in Seven-Card Stud. Two pairs are indeed a problem much of the time. Keep that in mind when you develop your plans. Have several plans in mind to handle the different situations when you catch the two pairs.)

Are you getting what I mean by having a plan? The above situations occur again and again. Have a plan ready to go for all of the most common hands that come along. With a plan already in place, you will be more relaxed, you will come across as a more competent player and your opponents will have more fear and respect for you. (A key concept to keep in mind is there are hands where you want to reduce the number of players competing for the pot—hands such as medium and big pairs. There are other hands, like straight and flush draws, where you want more people in the pot to make the pot odds correct for the drawing situation. For instance: If the odds against making or completing a flush are five to one, you need five other players in the hand to have the correct pot odds. In low-limit poker, it is often quite difficult to reduce the number of players by raising. However, it is usually cost-effective to try.)

And yet another example, suppose you catch this hand in Seven-Card Stud:

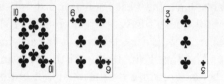

You immediately scan the board to count the number of clubs showing. You see two, neither of them face cards nor the ace of clubs. Should you play? You will be the last one to act. The betting comes back to you and there have been no raises. Yes, go ahead and call. Take a flyer at catching a high club on fourth street. If you should catch it you have a good shot at making the flush. However, on third street, if the pot has been raised before it gets to you, abandon the hand. This is just part of your plan. You will know exactly what to do under most circumstances.

PLANNING FOR "ROLLED-UP TRIPS"

"Rolled-up trips" refers to having three of a kind dealt to you, which happens once in a while. What is the best course of action? What plan will get you the most money?

Let me share my plan, which might help you develop your own. When I get rolled-up trips, I consider several alternatives, depending upon my position and the size of the trips. If the trips I get are nines or under, I will raise regardless of position. I want to cut down on the number of players. If the trips are tens or better, I will just call in early position. If the trips are tens or better and I am in late position, I might put in a raise. Usually, in low-limit poker, a raise from late position will not drive out players who have already put money in the pot. This puts more money in the pot. If I don't raise on third street, I will usually not raise on fourth street either. The reason for that is that I want the raise to come on fifth street where the bets are double (in a structured betting game). If I should make a full house on fifth street, I will very likely slow-play the hand until sixth street. I want all the draws in there so that I get more money.

PLANNING FOR TEXAS HOLD 'EM HANDS

Now, let's consider some hands in Texas Hold 'Em. My advice is to raise with any of the following hands, regardless of position:

These hands require that you do what you can to limit the number of players. Getting these hands heads-up is the ideal. The exception I will make, sometimes, is when I get the queens when I have placed the blind bet and therefore am the last to act on the first betting round, and there are quite a few players already in the pot. A raise won't drive many of them out, so I occasionally don't raise and will wait to see the flop. This move has some surprise factors also.

Playing the big pairs is pretty straightforward. However, what if you catch a big pair in late position and the bet is raised in front of you? What do you do? What is your plan?

My plan is to re-raise. I hope that I will get all the other players out and that I haven't run into the aces if I have the kings or queens. I will also have a better position than the original raiser, and that gives me more options than he has, after the flop.

Now, what would be your plan if you catch this hand in middle or late position?

Or this hand?

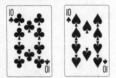

Or this hand in late position?

I suggest you visualize each hand and make a plan. When you have a plan for that pair of jacks, take a deck of cards, select out the two jacks, and start flopping three cards as the dealer would do. On each flop, reflect on how well your plan would work with that particular flop. Do this again and again and again. As you see actual situations, you might want to modify your plan or add to it. This practice is extremely valuable.

FLOPPING THE MONSTER HAND

The other day I had this hand in the blind:

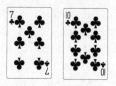

The flop came:

Wow! As the saying goes at the Hold 'Em table, "That's a pretty good flop for that hand." I'm sure I twitched a little when I saw a full house out there.

This is really where a plan becomes important. You will only have a nanosecond to act. You cannot give away the strength of your hand, because you want to maximize your potential win by building the pot, so what is the best course of action to top out the pot?

My thinking is that a flop like that is too big to bet. I want someone else to take a shot at it. I want all the players drawing for flushes and straights to stay in the game trying to make their hands. So I will check this hand. In this actual situation another player bet, and was called in two places before it got to me. I called. The next card was a king, the K♥. Not much help there unless someone made two pairs, kings over sevens. The cards I really wanted to see would be almost any diamond or a six, preferably a black six. The six of diamonds presents the very, very slim possibility of a straight flush. Anyone drawing at a straight would make their hand with a six. Any diamond might make someone a flush. A jack would also work, but there was a very slight danger of someone having a pair of jacks in their hand and making a full house with jacks full of sevens. The card I really did not want to see would be another ten. If someone had called with a ten in his hand, I would tie for the pot, with a full house of tens full of sevens.

There are many types of starting hands in Texas Hold 'Em. For instance, you should have a plan for where and when to play the medium pairs like eights, nines and tens; another plan for small pairs; one for high suited *connectors* (J♣-T♣, for example); big suited cards with a gap; big unsuited connectors; and medium suited connectors.

"CALLING A RAISE" PLAN

One very important strategy often overlooked by even intermediate poker players is knowing when to call a raise. What I am about to write may seem strange to you, but please trust me on this. The strategy: *You must have a much stronger hand to call a raise than to make the raise yourself.*

For example, in Texas Hold 'Em, in order to call a raise, especially from a decent player, you must have a big hand, preferably a big drawing hand like K♣-Q♣. I see it all the time where a person will call a raise with a hand like J♣-T♥. Against a raise, that jack-ten off-suit is trash. Some folks will even call a raise with a six-seven off-suit!

In Seven-Card Stud, you must also have a strong hand to call a raise. If a person with a queen showing raises, you must either have a better pair than the queens or a very strong flush draw. In fact, if you have the pair of queens beaten, you should re-raise!

My advice is to have a list of hands either written down or firmly in your head with which you can call a raise. Do not vary from that list until you have a whole lot of experience.

Is this planning stuff beginning to make sense for you? Whatever game you play, have a sketch in your mind of the best action to take.

Have a master plan already in place so your action is smooth, easy and powerful. Once you get a few of these plans in place, it will be easier to develop others on the spur of the moment.

THE 80/20 RULE

When you have a plan securely in place for several potentially big hands, you will then be able to revert to what I call the 80/20 rule. Since you never want to become predictable in a poker game, you should have alternative plans available. Those alternative plans are what I call my 20% strategy. Eighty percent of the time I follow my plan. Twenty percent of the time, I do something else. That allows me to appear erratic. I want confusion to reign in the minds of my opponents. I always want them guessing what I am doing. That way, I can depend upon them calling me when I have a big hand. They all think I play only strong hands, so I throw in a few red herrings to throw them off guard.

There is a bit of danger here for the newcomer to serious poker. The danger is that throwing in a red herring is much too attractive for a poker player. Many players overdo the 20% part. They love to play so much, they try to bluff or overplay a mediocre hand. They try to muscle through a hand against people who do not understand they are supposed to fold. My advice is to wait until you get pretty good at this game, until you have your 80% play well in place, before you start doing the 20% part. We all love to play, and that 20% move can become a snare that will trap you.

PLUGGING LEAKS

An important part of good planning to closely examine your game. One of the terms used for this examination is "plugging the leaks." Almost all players have some "leaks." Plugging those leaks not only saves money, but it also enables you to see how other players make similar mistakes. What you learn about yourself usually applies to other players. For instance, somehow I developed a love affair with king-jack off-suit in Texas Hold 'Em. I knew enough to not play king-ten off-suit except in very late position, but somehow I continued to play that damn king-jack. Sometimes I would even call a raise with that rubbish. Playing king-jack off-suit anywhere except in late position is a "leak." Even to this day, I am tempted to play that hand in middle position. I have grown to hate the hand.

We all have leaks in our game. Identifying and plugging those leaks are ongoing tasks. That is where planning comes in. Planning is taking the time to focus on how you play.

The choice of starting hands is a good place to start looking for leaks. Like that king-jack, for instance. Examine each starting hand carefully. One of the big no-no's in Seven-Card Stud is staying with a pair when another card of that rank is showing. Staying with three cards of one suit when four or more of that suit are showing on the board is a no-no. Tempting, yes. Smart, no. Definitely, these are leaks. But we must look deeper for the subtle leaks.

Similar to that junk hand of king-jack off-suit are other "habits" that can bleed your chips. I found another leak that I am still trying to remedy. I have noticed that in a Texas Hold 'Em game, my choice of starting hands in the early middle and middle middle positions is a tad weak. I am quite careful of the starting hands in early position. I am quite loose and aggressive with my starting hands in late and last positions. I will usually raise with any two face cards (I include the ace as a face card in this context) in late position if the pot has not already been raised. (Please refer to the definition of early, middle and late positions in Texas Hold 'Em.)

I confess that I have played some marginal hands from early middle and middle middle positions. Sometimes I have not gotten burned with a raise and sometimes I have been lucky and I have won money. However, in the long run, I am convinced I have played too many hands from those middle positions. I am speaking of marginal hands like a pair of sevens.

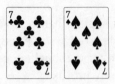

Or:

Now that is a REAL marginal hand in early middle and middle middle position.

Or:

Or:

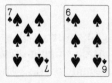

These are all playable hands in certain situations. In fact, I like those hands a lot in late middle and late positions. Sometimes these are raising hands. There is nothing wrong with the cards, only my position in the betting.

When I realize I am playing too many marginal hands from marginal positions, I can modify my play. When I·give some serious thought to my play, I can come up with these thoughts and make the modifications necessary to restore my profits.

Leaks After the Starting Hand

The leaks harder to identify occur later in the hand. Suppose you are in a Texas Hold 'Em game and you start with a pair of sevens in late position in an unraised pot.

The flop comes:

Let's analyze what you have or, in poker jargon, "where you are at in the hand." You have an overpair and an inside straight draw. What should you do when the action gets around to you? The blind, a nice lady named Sylvia, bets. That is to be expected from a blind hand with that *rag* (poor) flop. She could either have a four or a pair. However, she might also have a straight already made, either a two-four or a four-seven. Two people call her bet. What to do? There are three possible courses of action: a raise to help clarify the hand, a call, or throwing the hand away. You have a fair chance of having the best hand at the moment, and a raise might get out the players who would call one bet with overcards. However, there are many dangers. You do not want to see another seven hit the board. Certainly someone has a four and would make a straight. Also consider that you really don't want to see the seven of diamonds, which might give someone a flush. The best you can hope for in this situation is a black four to give you the straight. However, even a black four wouldn't give you the nut straight. Someone playing a seven-eight would have you hammered. Remember also that someone could be holding a pair of eights or better and have not raised before the flop. Do you see the leak? Calling before the flop with that pair of sevens was okay. Continuing to play them after the flop and the betting action that gave an indication of the strength of other hands would be money poorly invested.

This is where planning comes in. When you have taken the time to focus on your play while relaxing at home, you can run a scenario like this in your head. Instead of having to decide on the spur of the moment, when the tension is high, you have a plan already in place. You have identified that pair of sevens as a leak under these and similar circumstances. You can quickly identify the dangers and make a good profitable decision.

The added benefit to this kind of planning is that now you can more easily identify the players who have not done their homework. Most players would call with that pair of sevens after the flop and lose a bunch of chips. Those players are just the guys you want to play with in the game of poker. It is an advantage to you to know who these players are and what they are likely to do under similar circumstances. If you find consistent behavior after the flop and on the turn card or on fourth, fifth and sixth street in

Seven-Card Stud, you can make better estimates of their hand strength. The more clues you can accumulate on each player, the greater your capacity to read them.

PLAN FOR OTHER PLAYERS' MISTAKES

I often play with a guy I'll call Jim. He loves to try to dominate people with loud talk and a threatening manner. He also has a tendency to bet and/or raise whenever the board flops a pair in Texas Hold 'Em. This betting action indicates he has three of a kind. Of course, he seldom has what he is representing, but he has won quite a number of pots with this tactic. He has also paid off the people who have really held the matching card.

When you spot a player like Jim, do some planning. You can take advantage of his play. For instance, if he is sitting to your left, and you can get him heads-up or with one other person, a check-raise might drive him off the pot. You have to be very selective when you do this. Why? Because you can run into a player who has the three of a kind, or you might do it when Jim has gotten lucky and he has the three of a kind. I like to have some outs when I do the check-raise. I want to have a flush or straight draw so if I run into a set I can still draw out on Jim. A couple of times I have check-raised Jim with a draw hand and hit it. The look on Jim's face is precious.

Here is another situation where planning will pay off. Another player I know, Robert, plays almost every hand. It doesn't matter what game it is, Robert will play. When the pot is checked to him, and he is last to act, Robert can be counted on to bet. It matters not that he has nothing, he bets simply because he is last to act and he sometimes actually wins the pot with a bet. Here is how I manipulate this situation. If I should be in the blind in a Texas Hold 'Em game and Robert is on my right and I have a hand like:

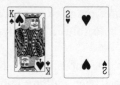

If the flop should come:

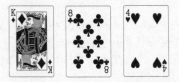

While I have flopped the top pair, I have such a poor kicker that I am afraid to bet. Anyone else who also has a king will have me beaten. I check and if it gets around to Robert, I know that he will bet. If anyone else bets, I will fold my hand. If Robert bets, I will simply call. Usually I will continue to check my hand and let Robert bet it all the way. I know if I should bet out, Robert would fold, since he is afraid of my betting. By allowing him to bet for me, I show a nice profit for the trash hand. However, if the flop came something like:

I would check as before, but when Robert bets, I would check-raise. Now I want to get information. I want to know who could be on a diamond draw. If a player calls two bets, you can be pretty sure he or she is drawing at the diamonds. If a diamond doesn't come on the turn, I bet. If a diamond doesn't come on the river, I will check unless I have made two pairs or three kings. If a diamond comes, I check and fold if the player bets.

Before I leave the Robert story, here is one more way I have figured out how to manipulate him. When I have nothing and I don't want him to bet, I simply look at him, smile and say as I check, "Robert will bet." When I do that he will never bet.

Do you see how a bit of planning allows you to squeeze out a few dollars from a poor hand?

Low-limit poker players make all sorts of mistakes that you can capitalize on. Lots of players will play if they have any ace in their starting hand, in both Seven-Card Stud or Texas Hold 'Em. They just feel compelled to play a rag hand like:

in Seven Card Stud or

in Texas Hold 'Em. Many times I have seen a Texas Hold 'Em player start with a very bad ace like that A♦-3♠, call a raise from a good player, catch an ace on the flop and RAISE with it. Now that is a mistake. When you find a player like that in your game, say a word of thanks. Those are fun players. It is a good idea to have a plan for players like that because when you raise with *Big Slick* (an ace-king in any combination of suits in Texas Hold 'Em) and catch an ace, that player will call all bets. It is truly harvest time.

One day in a Seven-Card Stud game, I found a guy who would re-raise with any buried pair, fives, sevens or even deuces. Once I caught on to what he was doing, I would cap off the betting when I had a pair of jacks or better. He paid me a lot of money that day. He made three of a kind once, but fortunately for me I made a better three of a kind. When you find a player who makes mistakes, take just a moment and hatch a plan to take advantage of his or her mistake. Once you develop a plan, file it away and bring it out when you find another player prone to the same error.

PLAN FOR LOSSES

Regrettably, losses occur. That fact of life has to be considered and a plan developed. Sometimes the cards run against us, and we should have a clear idea of how many dollars we can afford to lose in a particular game. (I will also touch on this in the chapters on Money Management and Emotional Control.) For the beginning and/or recreational player, certain limits should be in place. For instance, in my opinion, if the game is a $2–$4 limit game, a loss limit of $100 to $150 is reasonable. In a $3–$6 limit game, maybe go up to a $200 loss before you call it quits. The reason for these loss limits is for you to have a possible recovery factor. If you get down $300 in a $2–$4 game, you don't have a likely chance of getting even. I have found that sometimes those darn cards just don't turn around.

I am not saying it is easy to accept a loss and get up and quit. It is very tough to do. Some players, even quite experienced players, go into a panic when they get stuck. They begin to play fast and loose trying to get even. Therefore you should have a definite figure in mind as your loss limit. When you arrive at that loss limit, get up and leave. Take the loss, because your mind-set is not positive, and that also works against you. A negative mind-set is very detrimental. Getting good hands beaten again and again is tough to take. When the game ceases to become fun, it is time to quit for the day. Later on in your poker career, you will certainly have a different approach. The loss limit is a safety net for you for the time being.

PLAN TO LIMIT PLAYING TIME

It is a good idea to plan how many hours you will play in any given session. I find that my focus starts to dim after six or seven hours. My game begins to slip after that. However, I am not committed to play that number of hours. I have four criteria for quitting before my allotted time:

1. If three unusual things happen that beat my good hands, I will quit or find another place to play. I have found that two peculiar events do not affect me. However, that third one seems to make me lose my normal good humor and changes my outlook on the game. So I quit, regardless of how many hours I have played.

2. If the lineup in the game changes to where I am not the favorite. I always want to be the best player at the table. If several loose players are replaced by several tough players, I will quit or try to find a better game with a higher chance of winning. I have found that the greater the number of loose players at my table, the greater my hourly win rate.

3. If I should go on tilt (lose emotional control). It happens rarely these days, but I still keep the option open.

4. Once in a great while I will actually get tired of the game. When I have to force myself to keep playing because I haven't played the set number of hours, I will also quit.

There are only two reasons for me to extend my playing hours:

1. When I am running extremely well, I will stay around an hour or so beyond my time limit. However, I will place a close watch on myself and my chips. If I feel the cards turning against me, out I go. If I feel I am still sharp and excited about the game, I will become a tad more conservative and continue to play.

2. Once in a while, in a very good game, when I am about even, and I am just not catching good cards, I will extend an hour or so. I am hoping to catch just one hand to make the day into a good win. This is one of the few times I will bend the rule about how many hours to play just a click or two.

7

EMOTIONAL CONTROL

OF THE FOUR CORNERSTONES, emotional control has perhaps the most profound impact on the outcome of your game. When you lose your control, you can lose big time. When you can maintain control, your winnings will be more consistent. Here is a story of how I let my emotions get the better of me.

I was in my first year of playing poker. The game had modest limits of $4–$8 and it was Seven-Card Stud, High/Low Split, 8 or better to qualify for low. I was deeply engaged in learning this game and learning how to play poker in general. The pot was good-sized and I had a pretty decent hand and thought I would win at least half the pot and maybe the whole thing. A player across the table got a miracle card and won both ends of the pot. As he was stacking his chips he looked at me and said something sarcastic about my play. Smoke rings started to come out my ears, and I just about jumped across the table to take him on.

The end of the story is that I didn't do anything physical, but I sure learned a lot from that experience. The player who said those things to me was experienced enough to know that he could make me go on tilt, which is basically to become angry enough to where I lost all sense of rational thought. He wanted me to tilt out so he could take more of my money, which he succeeded in doing.

However, he taught me a lesson that I cherish to this day. That lesson is emotional control.

The Elmer Story

I was in a low-limit game of Texas Hold 'Em. One of the other players in the game was a man I'll call Elmer. Elmer is one of the most irritating people you can meet. He reminds me of the scraping sound of a nail across a blackboard.

A good player, Henry, came to the table. Henry is a middle-aged man who has great emotional control. On the very first hand, Henry was dealt the king and queen of clubs. He raised and drove Elmer out of the pot. The flop came all diamonds, queen high. Henry had flopped the top pair, but with a dangerous flop. Elmer laughed at Henry when he saw the flop, believing Henry would get beaten. Henry bet and got called by a fairly loose player. The next card off was another diamond. The other player checked to Henry and Henry bet. The loose player check-raised. Elmer laughed outright. What happened next was classic. Henry thought for a moment, looked Elmer in the eye and asked, "Do we know your next of kin?" Elmer blubbered and shut up for a long time. A lot of men would have gone on tilt because of what Elmer did. Not Henry. He just threw his hand away and went on to win a bunch of money, a lot of it from Elmer. That was a demonstration of how emotional control can make or break your concentration and your game.

The David Story

David was one of the very best local players here in Colorado. He went to The World Series of Poker held at Binion's Horseshoe in Las Vegas and did well. He decided that he would move to Vegas and play poker for a living. He did okay for a while. Then the reports started coming back that David was losing. He was playing in games that were too rich for him and it appeared he was over-matched. The next thing we heard was that he had moved to California and was playing in the big card rooms in Los Angeles. Then one day he appeared back here in Colorado, playing in low-limit games. And he was playing badly. His hand selection was poor, he was attempting to power bet the calling stations off the pot, which is an impossibility. Soon, David disappeared from the poker scene entirely. What happened to one of the best players? He lost his emotional control. He became convinced that he could be a great player and that any hand he chose to play could be powered into a winner. The really good players caught on to this and played demolition derby with him. The poor players didn't have any idea of what he was doing and called him down. That is an example of the loss of emotional control that is just slightly different from the first two examples.

TRIGGERS

Each of us has certain hot spots that set us off. It could be that guy on the end is just an obnoxious creep and we don't like his looks. When he rakes in a pot that should have been mine, I want to punch out his lights. He just grins and says something like, "I would rather be lucky than good." He is getting my goat, and he knows it.

I can be quite sarcastic when I want to be. I have been known to say something like, "What did you have on the flop?" when one of these clowns runs me down in a Texas Hold 'Em game. I got a pair of kings beaten once by a guy who had absolutely nothing on the flop, nothing on the turn and caught an ace on the river. He had a lousy A♦-4♣ that he stayed with all the way. He did not even have a draw for anything except an ace after the turn. It was a terrible play on his part, so I had to ask him, "What did you have on the flop? Or on the turn?" He just smiled and stacked my chips into his stacks. Stupid plays like that pull my trigger. What are your triggers?

Maybe the trigger is a couple of great drawing situations that did not come in and you are angry with the cards.

Maybe the trigger is the guy next to you blowing smoke in your face.

Maybe the trigger is a dealer you do not like, and you never win a pot when he is dealing.

These are but a few of many triggers. Find out what lights your hot spots and spend some time coming to terms with them. If you can identify what sets you off, you can make plans to defuse those triggers before they happen.

Frustration From Bad Cards

Many a player has been upset, or put on tilt, by a long run of bad cards. Players complain a lot about having to sit for an hour or so waiting for a decent starting hand. They moan and complain, they blame the dealer, ask for deck changes, change seats and tables. They will try several tricks to try to change the flow of the bad cards. The good player knows that long runs of poor cards happen, and he just sits back and waits it out. If you start getting frustrated and upset by the long run, you will be a prime target for the better players. They will try to get you to tilt. But simply fold your arms, sit back and wait. Tell yourself you are a good player and just wait out the bad run. Everyone gets a bad run now and then. It is one of the realities of poker.

One trigger that seems to affect a lot of players is when they do well in a poker game, rack up several stacks of checkers or chips and then run into a very dry spell. They have trouble coping with the swings that appear to be a natural part of the game. Suppose a guy sits down and wins a couple of hands. He loosens up a tad and plays a few more hands. He draws at a straight, makes it and wins the pot. He takes a long shot at making a flush, hits it and wins the pot. Things are going his way!

Then suddenly, without his necessarily being aware of it, the cards change. Now he draws at a straight and doesn't make it. He hits the flush but doesn't win the pot. Suddenly his chips are all gone. What happened?

This kind of turnaround puts a lot of players on tilt. The cards come your way, you win and then you come to expect the cards will keep coming. When they don't, you get upset. Unless you accept this phenomenon in poker, you could become quite frustrated, which will lead to big losses. The flow was favorable and then unfavorable. This up-and-down swing is the nature of poker. The cards will come back. In the meantime, you must tighten up, play only quality cards and keep a close watch on your emotions.

It should be noted that some excellent players claim that money moves around the table. What does that mean? It means that it is common for first one person and then another to get on a streak and stack up some chips. The money moves from one stack to another to another, etc. The idea for you is to catch some of it permanently as it moves around.

The Frustration of Being Second Best

Far worse than a long run of bad cards is catching pretty good cards and then getting them beaten. Getting half a dozen hands cracked that could have been winners is a problem few people can handle and keep their cool. In poker there are no silver medals— second best gets no rewards. Poker only pays off on first place.

The biggest problem with second-best hands is the cost. To get to this point, you would have had to invest money in the pot to get to the showdown. With just a few second-best hands, a nice win can turn into a devastating loss. Unlike a long run of bad cards, which doesn't cost you much because you fold (or should!) early on, second-best hands can bust you out of the game.

The way to cope with second best is solid and well-practiced emotional control. Two bad losses in a row get the process started.

After the second loss, tighten up your starting hand requirements even more. I like to get up and take a walk and stretch a little. I wash my face, call my wife, have a cup of coffee, try to change my attitude. When I get back to the table, I renew my resolution to not let the cards get me.

I recently polled some of my friends who are good poker players. I asked them if they knew any good player who complained about bad beats. They all agreed. The really good players don't even think about bad beats more than a second. They positively don't give bad beats a second thought. They simply go on with the game. Every hand requires a lot of concentration, so they don't have any extra brain cells to worry about how the bad beat occurred. Consistent winners worry only about the next hand, not the last.

Unrealistic Expectations

There is no doubt in my mind that much of our discomfort at the poker table is self-induced. Gosh, am I guilty! I want to win. When I invest my time, money and travel in a poker game, I am there to take home some money. I *expect* to take home some money. My records tell me that I have a very, very good chance to win. Somewhere between 78 and 79% of the time I will log a win. So, of course, I have expectations of winning. And when I don't win, I get irritated, because I feel I am supposed to win.

Therefore, expectations are also a trigger to set off emotions. Maybe they don't set off your emotions, but they certainly do some damage to my emotions. What I need to do to cope with these expectations is have a stern talk with myself. Do you do that? I do it all the time. I do it on the way to the game. I do it when I wake up in the middle of the night and certainly on the way home after a losing session. I have an internal dialog that is eloquent. I can call myself all sorts of names like dumb-dumb, numbskull, airhead, space cadet, etc. Those are the nice names, the ones I can put in print. And the more times that I win in a row and then hit the losing session, the tougher I am on myself. As I said, I expect to win.

I believe the best advice I can give myself is to relax and take a world view. By a world view, I mean to see my poker game from a distance. I can't expect to win all the time. No one does. Why should I? Therefore, I can set up a reasonable expectation of win rate. What percentage would I be happy with? Sixty percent? Seventy percent? Ninety percent? What would I be happy with? When I set up that expectation, a geography of wins if you will, I can view one or two losing sessions as to be expected.

Should I expect myself to be happy when I lose? No. Losing does not feel good. I want that money. I want the self-satisfaction of winning, of defeating the opponents. That is important to me. Therefore I cannot expect to feel good about losing. So if feeling good about losing falls outside my expectations, I can be okay with calling myself names while driving home after a loss.

Should I expect myself to learn from each losing session? You betcha. Losing is a great teacher. Losing motivates me. I review my play. I usually go to my computer and run a few thousand hands to sharpen my game. I review books that I haven't read for a while. I want that losing session to be productive.

Expectations can get us into trouble, but if we use our heads, we can make the adjustments to counter their influence. Again, most of the time it ain't easy, but if we want to make poker into a profitable enterprise and a great part-time source of income, we have to let our heads rule over our emotions.

Rules Violations

Once I got very irritated with a guy who folded out of turn. I was making a bluff bet against two players. The first one hesitated a bit and the second one threw his hand away. This made the first one rethink, and he decided to call me. If the second player had waited, I'm sure the first one would have folded and I would have won the pot. That violation of the rules (act in turn) caused me to lose some money.

Another example: A player, Ralph, bet and another player, Jerry, folded. Jerry then turned to the last player, Ed, and said, "You have to call him." That statement was a clear violation of poker etiquette. Ed, intending to fold, changed his mind, called and won the hand. Needless to say, Ralph was furious. He called for the floorman. Unfortunately, the floorman could only caution Jerry not do that again. Be careful you don't allow yourself to lose control over this trigger.

Irritating Players

In a recent game of Texas Hold 'Em, Homer, one of the most irritating guys I know, sat down on my right. I like Homer sitting on my right. He immediately tried his usual tactics of slamming in a raise and then glaring at the other players if they dared to call him. He was lucky right away; his first two hands at the table were big pairs.

One of Homer's tricks is to raise to "buy the button." By trying to buy the button, I mean when he is to the right of the designated dealer, he will raise with almost any hand, trying to force out the dealer and achieve the best position. When I next got the button, sure enough Homer raised. Remember, he is sitting just to my right. I happened to catch a pair of queens, so I re-raised. His move was perfect for my hand, because now I could get in the second raise and put real pressure on everyone who had previously called. Sure enough, it worked and everyone folded, even Homer! He turned his hand over to reveal 9♥-3♣. Then he said sarcastically, "I showed you my hand, now show me yours." I mucked my hand face down and said, "Go to hell." That was not very nice, but Homer is the kind of guy who doesn't deserve good manners. I won the pot from him and then he started in his verbal abuse.

The very next hand I caught A♦-T♠. Again, Homer raised.
Again, I re-raised. This time one other person called the double
raise. Homer called. The flop came:

I had the top pair with only a fair kicker. Homer bet. I almost
threw my hand away, but decided to call. The other person in the
pot did muck his hand. The next card was 6♦. Homer bet again. I
was not worried that Homer had a straight. But he might have a
set. I called. The last card was the T♣. I had made the top two
pairs. Homer bet and I noticed he only had one betting unit left,
so I raised. My thinking was that if he had the set, he could not re-
raise because he had no money left. If he had A-K, A-Q, or A-J, I
would win the pot, and get all of his money! Homer called and he
showed me the A-Q. He had the best hand up until the last card,
when I drew out on him. Was he steamed!

Fortunately, there are not many people like Homer. I have
found there are many, many more very nice people than there are
guys like Homer. You will be surprised how many truly good
people play poker and you will enjoy them. Once in a great
while, a guy like Homer will disturb the game. When he does, be
prepared.

I suggest that you do not respond verbally to guys like Homer.
Simply let your cards and betting do the talking. Learn the tendencies of these kinds of players and use those tendencies against
them. These guys will often try to bully the game and try to intimidate players. Continue to play your best cards and try not to
get upset if your good cards get run down. Homer and his kind are
good people to have in the game because they are so easily controlled and easy to read. As you gain more experience, you will

have a good time with these people. They will contribute substantially to your bankroll once you learn how to deal with them.

GET TIRED AND TILT

Another common trap is getting tired. Most of your poker opponents think they can play for hours on end without losing concentration and focus. I believe that thinking to be erroneous. If you play a lot, like four to five times a week, you will build up your stamina. If you play occasionally, you will get tired and could make some costly errors in judgment. One frequent thing that I encounter is that after I have played five or six hours, I start to lose my edge. If I have a tough beat, I notice that my temper starts to kick up. That temper is a dangerous passion. If I let that passion ferment a while, I could have a problem. My counterattack to my temper is to get up, go to the bathroom, get a cup of coffee and talk to myself. It is just a bad and expensive policy to let emotions start to lead me around. As I indicated, this happens most often after I have played a few hours and the strain of constant and close observation has begun to take its toll on my ability to keep my emotions under control.

Irritations

Playing poker can produce a lot of tension. We have a tendency to get quite involved in the game, and emotions can run high. When emotions are high, little things can irritate us lot. Like having a smoker sitting beside you who constantly blows smoke at you. Or a chronic complainer slowing down the game with his gripes. Or players who jump from one table to the next and back again. Or the dealer makes a goof that costs you some money. These and many, many other things can cause enough irritations to get you angry or frustrated or short of patience or whatever. Emotional control involves being able to handle all these problems with a sense of humor and composure. Don't let the idiots block you from having a fun and profitable session. Take the tough beats in stride, knowing they happen in all low-limit poker games. Take the flow of good cards and bad cards with the same feeling tone. Be impenetrable. Be impassive. Let the lesser players complain. Maintain total control and just wait quietly for your wins to come. Don't use force, use patience and good humor.

8

BASIC MATH

DO YOU REMEMBER YOUR HIGH-SCHOOL math? Can you add fractions? How about multiplying fractions? Did you take trig or calculus or geometry? Perhaps you have an advanced degree in mathematics. Well, if you do, you have a leg up on the rest of us poor slobs. Fortunately, you do not have to be a math geek to do well at poker math.

The average poker player, as he sits down to play, asks some fundamental questions, such as, "What hands can I play that have a decent (moderate percentage) chance to win the pot? What hands do I play that make me the favorite to win the pot? If I catch a draw hand, like a flush draw, what are the percentages that I can complete my hand and win the pot? What about a straight draw?" In other words, the player should ask, "What hands will win under normal circumstances and which hands should I stay away from?"

Consider a player at a game of Seven-Card Stud. He catches this hand:

Should he play? Does thathand have an acceptable chance to win the pot? Should he call the bet?

These questions appear to be straightforward. I can hear you say, "Well, Andy, is the answer yes or no? Don't beat around the bush, tell us what to do." Here is my answer: Yes and no. How's that? Here is part one of my answer: Yes, you can call that bet, but only under certain circumstances. Seldom will that pair of fours win the hand without improvement. What are the mathematical chances of improvement? Look at these figures.

In percentage terms, the chances of improving are approximately: 1% to catch four of a kind, 8% of improving to a full house, 10% of catching trips and 43% to improve to two pairs. Obviously, your best chance to improve is to make two pairs. However, will two pairs win the pot? That is an answer I cannot give. I will tell you this: I don't like it much.

The other part of my answer: No, you should not call that bet if:

- there is another four showing on the board
- there is a raise in front of you
- there is more than one person to act after you have acted
- more than one king is showing on the board

If any one of those situations is present, throw the hand away and wait for a better opportunity. That pair of fours is, at best, a marginal hand. If another four is showing in front of another player, your chances of catching that last four is somewhere between slim and none.

If there is a raise in front of you, the message that a raise communicates to you is that someone has a good hand, a better hand than yours. Get out before you lose money.

If more than one person is left to act after your action, it is best to abandon the hand. There is just too much danger that someone will raise behind you and you will have to throw your hand away and you will have lost that good money.

Remember, your kicker was a king. If you are to improve to two pairs, that king will be the likely candidate to make your two pairs. If there is more than one king showing, your chances are quite long of catching the case card.

Do you see how basic math applies? There are only four fours in the deck and four kings. If you can account for most of them, don't give good money away trying for a low percentage chance of improvement.

Now let's put a different spin on that same hand, the 4♣-K♠ & 4♦. Suppose you had the pair of fours in the hole so it looked like this:

That is an important difference. Again assuming that no other fours were on board, not more than one king showing, and there is no raise in front of you, you could call the bet from an earlier position, say with no more than three people left to call. The difference is in the win potential of that buried pair. If you should catch a four on the next card, no one would be aware that you have picked up a powerful hand. You are now in a position to bet or raise and your opponents will not have a good idea of what you are betting on. You will also have about a 33% chance of making a full house. That full house will defeat any straight or flush and they will call all your bets, which will increase your chip count considerably.

A POPULAR POKER QUESTION

We have been talking directly and indirectly about where certain cards are located, either exposed, in someone's down cards or still in the deck. It is assumed that if you don't see the cards they are considered "live." Is this a logical conclusion?

Suppose we have been dealt three hearts in the first three cards in Seven-Card Stud. We immediately count the hearts showing and see only one. Now, four of thirteen hearts are accounted for, leaving nine hearts available to complete the flush. The game is seven handed so there are twelve cards dealt face down that we have not seen. If we assume even distribution of the hearts in those twelve unseen cards, we can account for three more hearts. However, all nine of the hearts might be in those twelve cards, leaving no hearts available to complete the flush. Or no hearts in those twelve, right? There is just no way to know. We certainly can say that distribution of the cards does contribute to the completion of a draw hand. That is one way to look at drawing situations. Here is another way:

Suppose you had been dealt the 6, 7, 8, 9, all different suits. You would need either a 5 or a 10 to complete the straight. You have seen three 5s and one 10 folded. That leaves four cards that will complete your straight. Take a deck of cards, select out the 6, 7, 8, 9 and the three 5s and one 10 that were folded. Now spread the remaining cards face down on the table and draw one card. What are your chances that you will draw a 5 or a 10? Four chances in forty-four, correct? Or one chance in eleven. Even if you took away forty-three of those cards leaving only one card, the chances are still the same that the remaining card is the one you seek. What I am saying is that random distribution is just that, random. Sometimes you miss and sometimes you catch, but mathematically it is always one chance in eleven. An unknown card is the same as any other unknown card.

Basic math helps you coordinate good playing and betting strategies. You will note it doesn't take a rocket scientist to work with these percentage figures. It just takes some effort to memorize certain basic percentages.

PERCENTAGES OF THE DRAW HAND

Let's consider staying with hands that occur frequently in Seven-Card Stud. Suppose you are dealt a hand like this:

Should you call the bet? That looks like a pretty good hand. Is it worth investing in? Because I used up my yes-and-no answer last time, let me answer these questions with "seldom." When you are dealt that hand with three low spades, throw it away if there are three other spades showing on board, perhaps even when there are two spades showing. Never, never call a raise with that hand. Never call with that hand when you are in early position. When you catch that hand in late position and you can get in cheap and there are no more than two spades showing and there are at least four other callers, go ahead, take a shot at it. On third street your chance of completing a flush is a tad over 18%. Why do you want several callers? Since your chances are only 18% for completing the flush, you want to have enough money in the pot to make it profitable. If you do not catch a spade on the next card, preferably the ace or the king, throw the hand away. Why? Your percentage chance of completing the flush has dropped to about 11%. Those odds are too long to shoot for. It is bad math to call. However, if you should catch a spade, say the jack of spades, your chances of making that flush are about 47%, which is not bad. Now you only need two other people contending for the pot to justify calling. Do you see my reasoning? Since you have a good chance to make your flush and stand a good chance to win the pot, even with a low flush as described above, you will get a pretty fair return on your invested dollar. Once in a while you will lose to a higher flush, but you will have all the straights covered and the three-of-a-kinds beaten. The big danger is losing to someone who has stayed with two pairs and hits a full house.

Basic math works. Please invest some time in thinking about how it works and why you should spend some time learning a few percentages. When you grasp those percentages, translate them into figuring how many players it takes to be active in the pot to justify your participation.

9

OLD BUT TRUE AXIOMS

As you are learning this marvelous game, please consider some wisdom that has been passed on by the generations of poker players who have gone before us. Many smart people have gone before us, and I think it is a good idea to listen to them and consider what we can learn from them.

AXIOM #1: HAVE THE BEST HAND, THE BEST DRAW, OR GET OUT

I like this axiom a lot because it helps me counteract that terrible drive that I have to compete for the pot. When I get in there and mix it up, sometimes I win. That winning is dangerous because I might get the feeling I can win any time I want. So for my personal game of poker and my betting strategy, I remind myself of this old principle: Have the best hand, best draw, or out. I draw a lot of my examples from the students I have had in poker class. One lady, Ellie, took my Seven-Card Stud class with her niece. Ellie was dealt three diamonds for her starting hand. She had the queen of diamonds showing. Her next card was the queen of spades, causing her to visibly jerk and smile. What she failed to notice was that the fellow across the table now had a pair of kings showing. The dealer pointed to the man with the pair of kings and said, "Check or bet." He bet. When the action got around to Ellie, she studied his kings, looked again at her hole cards and her pair of queens and called his bet.

I stopped the action right there and asked Ellie why she had called a bet when she was so obviously beaten. She replied, "Because I might catch another queen."

This is what my wife, a professional teacher, calls "a teaching moment." Circumstances handed me the opportunity to demonstrate a powerful concept. So I wrote king-king on the board. Then I wrote queen-queen on the board. Then I asked Ellie who wins the pot if neither of them improved their hands. Ellie admitted that he would. I asked who would win if both improved to two pairs or three-of-a-kind. Everyone agreed he would. I reminded the class that the only way for Ellie to win was if she got luckier that he did. He had exactly the same chance to catch a king as she did to catch a queen to go to three of a kind. Of the three things that could happen to her, two of them were bad. At this point, Ellie said, "But I like to play." Right there is the story of most poker players. Consequently, most poker players are losers, some say as many as 95%. We just love to play the game, and we pay to play.

It is not only our love of playing that makes it tough to follow this axiom, it is that we don't want to quit if we are behind. This is a trait of human nature. Just because that other guy is ahead doesn't deter us. If we are playing in a football game, we don't quit when we get behind. The same is true in all other sports. I play a bit of tennis. I sure don't quit when I get behind. In fact, I play harder. We feel we can catch and beat the other guy. But in poker, trying to come from behind is incorrect thinking. We are paying good money to try to beat the odds, to *go uphill*, as poker players say. To go uphill consistently is to be a loser. Once in a while, okay, but as a practice, no. Listen to what the axiom is telling you. This axiom has some of the wisdom of the ages, the judgment of many generations of poker players. When you are second best, fold. Save your money for a better hand.

What about when you have a drawing hand? Some of the same wisdom applies. If you are drawing at a straight and it is apparent that an opponent has either made a flush or is drawing at it, fold. If you both make your hands, the opponent wins. The flush will beat the straight. In flop games like Texas Hold 'Em, it is easier to determine if you are drawing at the best hand than in Seven-Card Stud. In Hold 'Em, if you hold a hand like:

and the flop is:

You know you are drawing at the best hand. If any non-pairing club comes, you will have the nuts (best possible cards at that point in the game). No one will have a better hand after six cards. That is clearly having the best draw. Suppose you have this hand:

and the flop is:

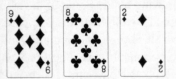

Do you have the best draw? No. There are two other possible diamond draws that can beat you if a diamond should come. Therefore this is a hand you should play, but carefully. Do not raise and think a bit about the bettor or raiser before calling. You no doubt noticed that you also had an inside straight draw.

AXIOM #2: RAISE OR FOLD

This axiom is one of the toughest to follow. The principle behind it is that you either have the best hand and raise, or you give it up. When playing low-limit poker, it is extremely difficult to determine who has the best hand. Players bet in wild and crazy ways. Some will raise with absolutely nothing. Some players will never raise, regardless of what they have. If they don't raise, you cannot tell if they have a good hand.

Very often you will be on a draw hand and there is just no possible way to know if your hand is the best draw. This is especially true in Seven-Card Stud. Take this hand, for instance:

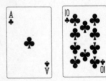

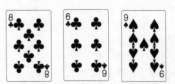

(in the hole)   (as your up cards).

You have a high percentage draw to make the flush and a small percentage draw to hit the inside straight.

Across the table from you is a person who has this *porch* (cards face up on the table).

The person happens to be an aggressive player. In the past he has raised with any kind of draw hand. You know that he loves to bet and/or raise with an intimidating porch. Should you call, raise or fold if he bets? You have counted a total of five hearts that are showing in other hands or have been folded. You can account for three clubs besides what you have. Is this a time to apply the axiom of raise or fold?

Let's take a close look at this situation because this kind of thing happens a lot. First, consider the amount in the pot. There is plenty of money in there to justify your own draw. There are three other people still active in the pot. So that is okay. If this guy has one heart with his hole cards, he has the higher flush draw. According to the number of clubs available compared to the number of hearts available, you have the better draw. If he has a king or queen in the hole, he has the better inside straight draw. However, you don't know any of this. You can assume he does not have an ace in the hole because he did not raise on third street, which would be his pattern. He could well have a small pair in the hole and he has picked up a heart draw. You have to give him credit for some good cards in the hole. But what are they? My guess would be that he has a king, a queen or a jack in the hole, maybe one heart. Now comes the test. What would you do?

Will you call his bet? Will you raise? Will you fold?

Quite often in poker you must use your intuition as well as your best guess. You may calculate the rational and mathematical probabilities and still go with your gut instinct, and sometimes you may be right. That is only one reason poker is such a fascinating game. Reason alone is usually the best way to go. Occasionally, inspiration is the better way.

My action in this example would be to fold the hand for several reasons. First, I give the guy credit for having some kind of cards in the hole. He may already have the flush, in which case I am beaten unless I draw the king or queen of clubs. That is too tough a draw. I also credit him with having a face card in the hole. That means his straight draw is better than mine. My only plus in this case is that I can account for more hearts than I can clubs: a small advantage because I have not seen the hole cards of the other players. All of my clubs could be gone, or maybe all the hearts could be gone. There is also a slim chance that one of the other three players will catch a full house or even a higher flush. My possible ace-ten flush is not that great. Since I certainly would not raise, I should fold.

How about another example? This one is from a $2 to $5 Texas Hold 'Em game. I catch a pair of queens in the single blind of $2. The game has become fast and loose, with three players having a raising contest. One of these loose players raises to $5 in middle position. What should I do? It appears there will be six players in the pot after this raise. I know that if I make a raise to $10, possibly one other player will drop. I also know that if I raise, it could set off a raising war that will cap off the betting costing each player $27. (Five raises were permitted at this particular card room.) I don't want to invest that much money on a pair of queens in the very worst position. What would you do?

I decided to call the extra $3 and decide what to do after the flop. If the flop came with cards lower than a queen, I would check-raise the original bettor.

The flop came:

Now what should I do? I checked, but knew that the raiser would certainly bet. It was checked to him, and he bet the $5. Two people called before I had to act. Should I raise or fold as the axiom calls for? Or should I call?

Let's do a little analysis. What do I know at this point? I know that the ace is a dangerous card. Several of the players at the table will play an ace with any kind of a kicker. That presents a big problem for that pair of queens. I also know the raiser did not raise to the maximum of seven dollars as he could have before the flop. This indicates he does not have a premium hand like ace-ace, king-king, ace-king, or ace-queen. He could, however, have two suited connectors or ace-ten suited. Any of these bigger hands would defeat my queens. Nonetheless, this player has a practice of raising with almost anything, like 4-3 unsuited! If that were the case I could have the better hand.

I decided that I could not raise, therefore I mucked (folded) the hand. It wasn't that I was so afraid of the raiser's hand, I was fearful of one of the other players having an ace. Maybe even an ace-three or ace-seven. My only real out was to catch a queen on the turn or river. Now suppose I called that $5 bet from the raiser. Suppose someone behind me did have an ace-three or ace-seven; he would certainly re-raise. The pre-flop raiser had the habit of re-raising whenever he was raised. Since I would not pay even $5 more to draw at a long shot, why would I go up to $10?

I hope these examples give you some help on how to analyze certain situations. If you have a poor hand, there is no predicament. When you have a great hand, there is no problem. It is only when you have one of those in-between hands that you have to do the hard work of thinking through possibilities and probabilities. Unfortunately, experience is often the only way to learn many of these factors.

AXIOM #3: PLAY TIGHT IN FRONT AND LOOSE IN BACK

This axiom refers to your position in the betting round. It is truly difficult to overstate the power of position. When you have good position, there are so many more circumstances that you can develop into winning conditions. You can manipulate the other players by playing strong, or what is called *power betting*, in the back line.

The reason for playing tight in front or early position is strictly for safety. You don't want to expose a moderate or marginal hand to a possible raise. Usually a raise indicates a powerful hand. You never want to go up against a powerful hand with a marginal hand, especially when they act after you. That is financial suicide. Whenever you are in early position and catch a hand that looks okay and you are tempted to play, ask yourself, "Can this hand withstand a raise?" If it cannot, toss it. Wait a hand or two and you will have the position. In very early position, you should only play hands that you can raise with. These hands are all premium hands and only come along once in a great while. It doesn't matter if you play in a fixed position game (all the flop games and draw games) or a random position game. In very early positions, your choice of starting hands is very limited: premium ones that you can raise with.

In middle position, you can loosen up just a tad. How loose is usually dependent upon the players in the game. If they are quiet and seldom raise, you can play a few more hands. If these players raise with most any kind of picture cards or draw hands, beware of modest hands. Remember, always try to have the best hand. Make them chase you, not the other way around.

Playing loose in back is the fun part of poker. You want to drive the other players a bit crazy and, when the cards are running for you, you can string them out like a cat plays with a mouse. Sometimes I will throw in a raise with the darnedest, weakest starting hand you can imagine. If you should hit it and show the hand down, the other players just look at you dumbfounded.

A very important concept to remember is not to invest a lot of money in a trash hand, even in late position, unless it improves substantially. If you call or raise with marginal or trash in late position, be prepared to dump the hand quickly. Don't get trapped or, as we say, "Don't get married to the hand." Many times, in a Texas Hold 'Em game, I will raise with nothing on the back line. If I hit the flop, I'll continue to bet. If I catch part of the flop, I'll continue to bet if I sense that the other players are weak. If I catch nothing on the flop, I might or might not bet. I will be looking for signs of weakness from the other players. If I perceive some, I'll bet to see what happens. You would not believe how many pots I have won with absolutely nothing. That is the power of position and the power of playing loose in back.

AXIOM #4: DON'T PLAY A HAND THAT, IF YOU MAKE IT, YOU CANNOT RAISE WITH

This axiom was given to me by an old-time poker player named George Kelly. George, an admitted conservative player, would be the first to admit there are exceptions to this rule. These exceptions would be found in the development of the last axiom. When you are playing loose in late position, you occasionally make some outrageous moves. Those moves don't count for this axiom. The idea of not playing a hand that you cannot raise with is for regular quality play. In other words, this axiom is for your usual style of play: tough, tight and aggressive.

Here is an example from Seven-Card Stud. Say we start with this hand:

Naturally there will not be any other eight showing and you are in good position and the pot has not been raised. You are hoping to catch an eight on the next card. However, on the next card, you catch the three of clubs. No help there. No one else catches anything either, so the hand is checked around. The next card you catch is the seven of spades. That is of some help, but the wrong kind. You are about to enter a trap. Another eight has been dealt to someone else, and another seven has also appeared. There is a bet. You did not catch the eight you needed to make a set and a real chance to win the hand. There are only two cards remaining in the deck that can help you. Two pairs, eights and sevens, is about as good as you can expect to get. So why call the bet? Could you hope the bettor has less than you have? No. Therefore you certainly can't raise. Remember, this is a structured game, so the bets double on fifth street. It is time to fold. Unless you catch a miracle card, you have no shot at winning. It was okay to take a shot at catching another eight, but when you didn't, you should not get trapped by some poor help, the seven. If you had caught another eight, you would have a raising hand, but you didn't, so the hand is over.

Here is an example from Texas Hold 'Em. Many players will play low connectors, suited and unsuited. Say you play this hand:

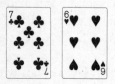

and you catch a flop like:

Looking around the table, you notice you have flopped the top pair (the sixes) along with a huge problem. Can you raise with your hand?

Let's take a closer look. What do you really have here? You have the top pair with a poor kicker. The big danger is someone with an overpair, like eights or nines. They probably would not have raised before the flop and will certainly raise now if you bet. Also you could run into someone playing a four-five. They have a straight already made. And then there is the real problem of people calling with overcards, say like a king-queen, and catching their card on the turn. You are playing a hand that you cannot raise with, which you shouldn't do. Dump it.

Playing low connectors, especially unsuited, too often creates real problems. Sure, we could catch a miracle flop and flop the straight. That kind of a flop will happen once in about 101 flops. You can't make much money drawing at those kinds of odds. Low suited or unsuited connectors is not usually a hand you can play and expect to raise with.

AXIOM #5: DON'T HOPE FOR CARDS

Hoping is the occupational hazard of poker. Hoping for a certain card to make a straight, hoping for any heart to make a flush. Hoping to catch the one card in the deck to make a wheel or a full house or a straight flush or whatever. Always, always hoping.

The absolute truth is that hoping, in the long run, is for losers. A winning player doesn't have to hope, because he knows the odds for catching a certain card or cards and he only plays when the odds are in his favor.

Texas Hold 'Em

Don't let all that verbiage above convince you that I do not get into hope situations. I wish I didn't, but I do. I was playing in a Texas Hold 'Em game and I was dealt this hand:

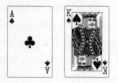

I raised the limit from late middle position and got four callers. I'm sure you could guess that I was hoping I would catch either an ace or a king on the flop. If I was really lucky, I would catch both an ace and a king. (That is about a 2% shot to catch two pairs.) What I got on the flop was:

I had flopped an inside straight draw with two overcards. There was no immediate danger of a flush since there were three different suits represented. It was checked to me and I bet the limit for three reasons; I had an inside straight draw for the best possible hand. Second, I had two overcards; third, I wanted to define the hand. I wanted to force out the weak hands, if I could. I got two callers, which is pretty average for that kind of flop. I was *hoping* they were both on straight draws also, say with a hand like Q-9.

Was I hoping for a queen on the turn card?

You bet. I know the chances of catching a queen either on the turn or river is about 16%. Any queen will make me feel good, but the queen of spades would be the best. Then it would not be possible for anyone to make a flush. I also know that I will probably win if an ace or a king would come on the turn or river. Besides, when I take the lead, as I did with the raise before the flop, I become the aggressor and I like to keep pounding. If I should get raised, I will back off and review the hand. I was *hoping* I could catch a queen and pull in that pot.

Beware of this hoping, if you can. Especially if you start to get involved with players who like to raise a lot. Sometimes these low-limit poker games get pretty woolly. If you should find yourself in a raised-up game where almost every pot is raised at lease once and quite often two and three times, your best protection against wild and crazy play is to call or raise with only premium hands. Even with premium hands, you will need to catch a good flop or, in Seven-Card Stud, an improvement on either fourth or fifth street. Don't get caught hoping in a wild game. Have the horsepower to blast these guys. You will find it only takes one or two pots in a raised-up game to show a very nice profit. That profit will come only if you can abstain from playing hope hands. Those hope hands will wreak havoc with your stacks. Play good cards and only stay around if you get some improvement.

What is intoxicating about these raised-up games is that quite often the wild guys who raise a lot will show down almost nothing and win the pot with it. You will think to yourself that you can get in there and gamble with them. My advice: Don't. These guys are chip burners. You should play a conservative game. Don't risk much money on marginal hands. Just play solid premium and wait for your opportunity.

Seven-Card Stud

We have all seen a certain development in Seven-Card Stud. Suppose you start with a hand like:

You are in late position and it only costs one betting unit to see the next card. You scan the board and note that there is only one king showing and two eights. It appears that most of your straight cards are still alive. On fourth street you catch the jack of hearts. Now you have one fair-sized pair and the same three cards to a straight. An ace and a nine have appeared, somewhat reducing your straight possibilities. You call one bet and get the fifth street card. You catch the 8♠. Now you have an inside straight draw, a three-card flush draw and a pair of jacks. This is typical of what happens in a hope situation. You started with a marginal hand and got in cheap. You caught a bit of help on fourth street and again on fifth street. You got suckered along to put more money in the pot. However, you are truly playing catch-up, hoping for that miracle card.

In a structured game of Seven-Card Stud, the bets now double. Should you continue to hope and call a bet or two? For the sake of the illustration, let's call this hand down. The next card you get is the ten of spades. Now you have a real trap! You have a draw at a straight flush! Any spade will give you a flush, any nine will give you a straight and the nine of spades will give you the straight flush. How can you not call?

By now you have lost track of how many spades have been exposed as well as if any other nines have been folded. The river card, seventh street, is the 4♠. You have the spade flush, queen high. The unfortunate thing is that an opponent has caught an ace high flush in diamonds and another opponent caught his card and made a full house. You end up in third place and forced to call all bets. That hope hand has cost you a bundle. You started marginally and got sucked into a whirlpool of expense. At no time did it appear that you were out of line. Each and every call seemed like the appropriate thing to do. However, do you recall the axiom "Raise or fold"? Do you see how that coordinates with the Hell of Hoping? At no time did you have a raising hand. Your hand was mediocre from the beginning to the end, so you got what you deserved. If you are playing catch-up from fourth street on, abandon the hand at fifth street when the betting limits double. That is the time to make the hard choice. Either have a raising hand or get out. Either have the best hand, the best draw, or abandon the boat. Poker can be frustrating if you allow it to control you.

RECREATIONAL POKER

Most home poker games have an invisible participant, a fun-loving, capricious lady known as Luck. She loves to visit a game and bless a player who doesn't understand anything about it, teasing them into thinking that they are really good at this game and they are set for life. This has happened so often, it has become known as "beginner's luck," though experienced players know it is the work of a Lady.

Although poker originated in America, it has traveled around the globe. I attribute much of that growth to the advent of games played at the family kitchen table. This is where we learn the real basics of the game. We learn that a flush is any five cards of one suit. We discover a straight is five cards with consecutive numbers, regardless of suit. We memorize the ranking of hands or "what beats what." A flush beats a straight, a straight beats three of a kind, etc. On this level, poker should be played for fun, with family members. It is often played without money, or for very low stakes (five or ten cents, quarter limits, etc.) But nevertheless, it is where we learn invaluable skills, and pick up both bad habits and good ones. There are lessons to be learned here.

The next logical step for some poker players is to proceed to the more or less regular poker game, which I call The Friday

Night Poker Club. By that, I am referring also to what some people call apartment games. There are so many different types of poker groups, it is impossible to try to describe each. Graciously allow me to group several under this one heading of The Friday Night Poker Club.

Although The Friday Night Poker Club is more serious than the kitchen-table game, it is still considered recreational play. We'll be discussing both of these games in this section.

10

KITCHEN-TABLE GAMES

IT IS AT THE KITCHEN TABLE that we discover the excitement of "wild cards." Wow! If deuces are wild, a single low-ranked two can change your hand from nothing to a winner. What an exciting concept to add to the game. This idea was certainly planted by Lady Luck to encourage participation in the home game. Now Grandma can play and win. Aunt Harriet would now rather play poker than gossip. The use of wild cards took an unexpected turn when players started making a lot of cards "wild." Someone invented Woolworth and made all fives and tens wild. Someone invented Baseball, where all threes and nines are wild. Along came Spit in the Ocean, where the dealer, upon command from any player, would turn over the top card and all cards of like number were declared wild. Another game that could be dealt has all deuces, red fours and one-eyed jacks wild. High Spade in the Hole became popular as a variation of Seven-Card Stud. The high spade that someone had face down won half the pot. There is no question, wild cards add excitement to the game. Maybe Lady Luck devised some or all of these games. As I said, she is capricious.

WILD CARDS

Let's take a closer look at the invention and use of wild cards in a game of poker. There is no question that wild cards add to the zest of the game. However, the price that is paid for the excitement is the increase in the luck factor and a decrease in the proportion of skill. Maybe this was exactly what Lady Luck was trying to achieve. More luck, less skill. I am not saying that wild card poker is without skill, but the use of wild cards dramatically changes the mathematical probabilities and consequently changes the *proportion* between skill and luck. It is a totally different game when one is drawing for the only card in the deck that will make a hand a winner vs. several cards that could do the trick.

Anytime there are a number of cards in the deck that will dramatically change the action, you have more people trying to catch a miracle card to make them the winner. Suppose you are drawing for a flush in Seven-Card Stud with deuces wild, and you have this hand:

Let's figure out how many cards will help you make the flush. Of the thirteen clubs, you have four. That leaves nine available. However, you can see four clubs in other hands. That leaves five clubs either in the deck or face down in someone else's hand. Assuming you will win if you catch the other club, you can catch one of five clubs or one of three deuces. That gives you eight chances to win. You also can catch two consecutive miracle cards and make a royal flush and you will certainly win.

So instead of having just one of five cards (the clubs) that will make you a winner, you have almost double the number of flush cards possible.

Suppose you have this hand, again in Seven-Card Stud, with deuces and one-eyed jacks wild. (One-eyed jacks are the jack of spades and jack of hearts):

Now let's figure out how many cards can help make this hand a winner. Obviously, any one-eyed jack or deuce will make a royal flush. Any diamond will make a very high flush, and there are seven (not counting the jack of diamonds or deuce of diamonds) that will make the flush. So add the seven diamond cards plus the four deuces plus the three jacks that will make either a royal flush or an ace-king-queen flush. That is a total of 14 cards that will make a good hand.

With all the possibilities, is it any wonder that everyone stays in to see if they can catch the miracle card and win the pot? Even when you start with trash, a couple of wild cards can turn your hand into a winner.

Say you have this hand in Seven-Card Stud with deuces wild:

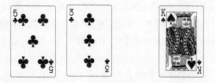

Now who in the world would play that trash? At the kitchen table, almost everyone. Suppose you catch the four of clubs on the next card. Then you catch a deuce. Now you have a straight flush draw.

Sure you have to catch a perfect card, but why not stay around and see what happens? You have two cards yet to come. How many cards will help you? The 6 ♣, 7 ♣, A ♣, along with any deuce will bring you home. Wilder things have happened, and what fun you will have showing your friends and/or relatives a straight flush.

Let's take another look at that same trash hand:

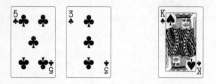

Now also suppose you catch a deuce on the next card. You not only have the straight flush draw, you have the possibility of catching another king along with another deuce. It is even possible to make five kings.

HOME GAMES ARE SOCIAL EVENTS

Poker, by its very nature, is a cutthroat game. The idea is to annihilate your opponents and take all of their money. I would check-raise my mother if she were in a game with me. Poker should be played with a bloodthirsty desire to draw and quarter the opponents. Except for cheating and physical intimidation, almost every tactic is legal. It is perfectly okay to lie to them. We can use every means to deceive them. It is fine to use any mental and psychological device to gain an advantage. This is the nature of poker. A friend of mine once said, "It matters not whether you win or lose; what matters is whether *I* win or lose."

Kitchen-table poker is usually played with family and friends. But how can I be nice when I am trying to deprive them of every cent they have? How can I be mean to my sweet Grandmother

Edith? She is quiet, never raises her voice, bakes me my favorite pie and loves me a lot. Uncle Wayne is usually three sheets in the wind when the poker game begins. Should I try to get him mad so he will go on tilt, or should I be nice?

The heart of the "problem" is that kitchen-table poker is a social event. It is supposed to be entertaining, an opportunity for families and close friends to have some fun. Real poker, straight poker, casino/card room poker, is for blood. So try not to exterminate your opponents in a home game. A serious poker player can still have fun if he or she can suppress the urge to kill. In fact, you can develop some very important skills, one of which is diplomacy.

Why practice diplomacy? It is a matter of deception. The idea is to laugh and joke with your opponents and make them feel good about playing with you. But make no mistake, this is duplicity pure and simple. You will be doing your absolute best to take all of their money. In order to do that, you usually want to be congenial so that they will stay longer and will return more often. Even when they are losing money to you, you want them to like you. Be sympathetic to them when they lose the pot. Offer them a "bad beat" chip or, as some people call it, a "good luck" chip. It takes some of the sting away from the loss. Tell them how you managed to "get lucky." Reinforce the idea that you just happened to get some fortuitous cards and managed to win by luck alone. That will give them hope that they will be the next recipient of favor by Lady Luck.

An important element of diplomacy is to compliment others when they win a pot. This goes far beyond saying, "Nice hand." If they had good cards and played them well, say, "You played that hand perfectly." Or you could say, "How did you know that you had Mom beaten? You played like you could see what cards she was holding." Another favorite phrase of mine is, "You maxed out that hand. Good job." These should be honest and sincere compliments; save the sarcasm for the card room.

This is a good place to practice your emotional control as well. Remember that poker is an emotional game. Be sure not to lose your cool and belittle someone. It is easy to become overly involved and say something that will hurt feelings. Always be charming and gracious.

A Couple of Don'ts

Don't mix alcohol and poker. This a very, very good rule for any kind of poker game, be it at home or in Vegas. Alcohol dulls your edge and clouds your judgment. In a serious poker game in a casino/card room, you could lose some of your ability to think straight and read players correctly. In a home game, alcohol could make you lose your patience and emotional control. You could easily slip and say something that should not be said to members of your family.

Cheating—This is another big no-no. I devote a separate chapter to cheating near the end of the book, but something must be said about it here. For the life of me I do not understand why anyone would cheat. This is especially true in a home game. Cheating must give some kind of an emotional reward, because the financial rewards are incredibly low and the dangers are absurdly high. If you are found cheating in a home game, your credibility is destroyed. No one will want to play with you. To be found cheating in a casino/card room is unforgivable, and you will be banned for life. However, I think it is worse to be caught cheating in a home game. You will be labeled dishonest by the people who mean the most to you.

It takes a lot of effort, thought and practice to be a cheat. If that same effort, thought and practice were applied to learning the correct way to play poker, you would have a lifetime source of income.

KITCHEN-TABLE STRATEGY

I have been telling you that playing poker around the kitchen table is a social event, where you should not try to slaughter the opposition.

But if you are playing in an apartment game with casual opponents or in the casino/card room setting, have no reservations about ravaging anyone in the game. The home game is different. The focus is still on winning, but winning with diplomacy and compassion. In a casino/card room, your goal is to kick butt and take names. In the home game you allow them a measure of respect and clemency.

Within the limited framework of these restrictions, you can also apply some strategies that will allow you to be a consistent winner. In fact, a home game is an ideal place to test out some systems, and to begin to apply what you have read in the previous section on patience, position, planning and emotional control. That kitchen table will provide you with an arena to experiment with some ideas, and the cost is much less than it would be in the card room. Being a consistent winner in a home game is not a problem for your table image if you win graciously. You will certainly gain the respect of your family and friends.

Suggested Tactics

Solid play, of the type you should employ in a casino or card room, will be almost impossible. Because of the use of wild cards, you will stay in more often, draw to some crazy hands that would be terribly unprofitable in the casino, and often play just to be a part of the fun. For instance, it is almost impossible to get a good fix on what the odds are for certain draw hands. Let me illustrate this with some statistics from Five-Card Draw High.

If you are using a regular 52-card deck, the odds of being dealt a straight in the first five cards are 254 to 1 against. In plain words, you will be dealt a straight once in 255 hands. (That is just a mathematical statistic for comparison only. It is possible to go a thousand hands or more without being dealt a straight or you could be dealt a straight in two consecutive hands.) If you include the "Bug" or Joker, which can be used with aces, straights and flushes, the odds against being dealt a straight in the first five cards is down to 139 to one.

A flush is dealt in the first five cards once in 510 hands. With the Joker, a flush is dealt once in 368 hands. You can see the incredible difference that happens with the use of only one wild card. When you have four wild cards, the odds change dramatically. When you have six or eight wild cards, who can figure it? A mathematician perhaps, but even he couldn't do it in the heat of the game.

When I play in a home game, I almost totally disregard the odds and just play for the fun of seeing what crazy possibilities happen. I forget about figuring the odds and just enjoy how the cards affect the people.

Practice Reading People

One important skill that is incredibly important for becoming a winning player in all types of games is developing your "reading" skills. Reading is predicting how powerful your opponents' hands are by noticing the way they play those hands. If they raise, you can estimate what they are holding by considering what cards are showing on the table (their porch), their position relative to the bettor and what their overall tendencies are. If they are wild and crazy players, a raise could mean almost anything: a stone cold bluff, a draw, or even a royal flush. If, however, they are conservative, a raise is a strong indication of power. How much power, then, becomes the question. Do you have a chance to beat them? Are you on a powerful draw? Do they understand the game well enough to realize the raise sends the appropriate message?

If your conservative and patient mother re-raises with a strong porch, you better consider that raise a real threat. If you do not have a powerful hand, get out.

Practice Reading the Cards

Another exercise, in addition to reading the players, is the discipline of reading the cards. If you watch closely what is happening with any particular group of cards, you can often save yourself some money or make astute raises to get more money in the pots you win. The obvious cards to beware of are the flush cards. If three of a suit are showing in someone's porch in Seven-Card Stud, a warning bell should ring telling you to beware of the flush. When that bell goes off, it is a good idea to count the other cards showing of that specific suit. (Another tip: If one person has a flush, sometimes more than one flush occurs in the same round of play. Can you figure out why that might be?) If you can count six or more of that suit showing in other exposed hands, the odds are against the player having a flush. Why? If one person has three of a suit showing and six others are showing in other hands, making a total of nine cards of that suit, that opponent must have two of the four remaining cards to complete the flush.

Again, in Seven-Card Stud, if an opponent is showing four cards to a straight like this:

You should automatically count the sevens. If you can account for three of the sevens, the odds are long that the person has a straight. If you can find only one seven, beware of the straight, especially if the game is played with wild cards.

Another Tip—Whenever you play with wild cards, and you have a full house, beware of being beaten with a bigger full house or four of a kind. Always, always count the wild cards as they appear. Those wild cards are fundamental to winning. Those wild cards hold the key to very good hands. Another tip is to be aware that when you don't see the wild cards, they will likely be hidden in someone's down cards (in Seven-Card Stud).

Bluffing

Bluffing and poker are synonymous in the minds of some people. Bluffing seems to attract the romantics. When my friends ask me about poker, it is almost always about having a "poker face" and bluffing. Many novice players believe that bluffing is a vital part of poker. The next time you play poker, keep track of the number of times the players bluff or try to bluff. Most important, notice how many times a bluff succeeds. Each poker game is different, so you will have to make a judgment on how often you should bluff.

Bluffing in low-limit poker is often overdone. I will seldom bluff in a low-limit game. The circumstances will have to be exactly right, otherwise it is usually a waste of money. If you are playing for pennies or matchsticks, forget bluffing as a winning strategy. The way you become a winner in a home game is by showing down the best hand. You will very seldom fool anyone into folding, because the stakes are usually low, and most people are in it for fun so they end up playing trash hands just for the hell of it. The only time I will bluff is when I am convinced that the one opponent still active is drawing at a straight or a flush and I have an indication he has missed. Then I will throw out a bet. If they did miss, they usually are just disgusted and will sigh, look again at their cards and then muck the hand. I usually support the bluff with a statement like, "This is the last time I am going to bet" or "If he (she) folds, I'll win this hand." For some reason those statements seem to work for me.

11

THE FRIDAY NIGHT POKER CLUB

THERE ARE TWO TYPES OF regularly scheduled, serious poker games. I call one of them The Friday Night Poker Club, while the other I term the apartment game. The organization of The Friday Night Poker Club is often a bit more tightly controlled because it consists mostly of regular players who know each other well, like neighbors, or colleagues from work, or members of a softball team or whatever. They occasionally allow guests, like a close friend of one of the regulars.

Apartment games are somewhat different because they often have one or two people who organize the game. These people rent an apartment and provide the table, chips, food and drinks. They also function as the banker. Some even lend money or "put it on the books." Some take checks and others operate on a cash-only basis. Some groups *rake the pot* (take a small percentage) to pay for the refreshments, cards, sandwiches, etc. Most Friday Night Poker groups do not hire a center dealer; they simply pass the deal. That is much cheaper, but there is also a price to be paid in pass-the-deal games; the games are slower and cheating is more prevalent.

Apartment games, like the Poker Club, have several regulars who seem to attend every game, but because they happen more frequently, they often have more casual, occasional players. Please be aware that apartment games are illegal in some communities, so check local laws before you attend one or try to organize one.

The personal interaction between players in The Friday Night Poker Club and the apartment game is very different from that in kitchen-table poker. For one thing, most kitchen-table poker games are family or social events. Seldom is The Friday Night Club or the apartment crowd made up of family members.

Some apartment games hire a center dealer, and you are expected to tip the dealer when you win a pot. Having a center dealer speeds up the game and reduces the chance of cheating. However, the presence of a center dealer does not ensure that cheating will not happen. Let me give you an example. I was invited to an apartment game, and I knew several of the players and the center dealer. The center dealer's son was a player in the game, and he and his father took turns dealing and playing. After an hour or so, when the dealers were changing places, I picked up the deck they were using and *riffled* (rapidly viewed) the cards, watching the corners of the deck. What I saw was what experienced players call *going to the movies*. The deck was a marked deck. Instead of the pattern staying the same through the riffle, the pattern changed rapidly. This happened because there were small, almost unnoticeable marks placed in the corners to identify the cards. The dealer and his son had purchased a marked deck and were able to read the backs of the cards as well as the fronts. I, and the other players, were being cheated. I left the game immediately, and that dealer and his son have a soiled reputation. Be aware and be careful.

ADVANTAGES OF FRIDAY NIGHT POKER

There are some wonderful advantages to The Friday Night Poker Club games. For one thing, these games are much cheaper than playing in a casino/card room. There is usually no rake except for the refreshments. When the casino takes $3 to $5 off the table for each deal, a lot of money disappears. But the cost of playing poker is considerably lower at The Friday Night Game. No money is lost to the house.

Another important, positive, feature of The Friday Night Poker Club is the camaraderie. I have developed several really close friendships because of my involvement in these games.

The astute poker player will also find that these games can be lucrative. It is possible to earn a nice, supplemental income and have a great time doing it. Another advantage of The Friday Night Poker Club, one that you can turn into cash, is that because you are playing with regulars, you can get a very good fix on the tendencies and tells of the other players. You will learn how each person is likely to bet, how they give away their hands, etc. Those tendencies and tells turn into cash for the player who will focus on and study his opponents.

The Friday Poker Club often provides a way to learn some new and interesting poker games. There are some challenging variations on poker that are played in these groups.

DISADVANTAGES OF FRIDAY NIGHT POKER CLUBS

Belonging to the gang that meets for poker on a regular basis does not mean that everything is always friendly. I have seen some fierce arguments at some of these Friday Night games. Let's look at some of the reasons, and then I'll offer some advice on how to prevent these problems from occurring.

Rules Interpretation

Quite often there is a disagreement over the rules, or the interpretation of those rules. Seldom is there a group that appoints one person to referee disputes. That is clearly one advantage of a casino/card room. The floorperson at the casino/card room has the final say when a decision has to be made. Since that floorperson has no personal conflict of interest because of friendships, it is believed he will give an unbiased decision. If you have been involved with a disagreement in a home game, you know exactly what I am writing about. It can get pretty ugly. Friendships are broken, guys don't speak to each other, some people end up leaving the group and the atmosphere is terribly tense. At these times, it is certainly not fun.

Therefore, a very good solution is to write out the rules agreed upon by everyone in the game; then each player should be given a copy. New players, including one-time guests and occasional players, should be given a copy of the rules when they enter the game and told that these are the rules of this particular game. When the rules take a written form, they are more readily accepted.

If there is still a conflict, or if there is some disagreement on what rules to write down, then it is a good idea to appoint a parliamentarian, or someone to research and become knowledgeable of the traditional rules of poker. If a dispute should arise, that person is called upon to determine the correct action. This should help to make everyone feel more comfortable and enjoy the game a bit more.

Recruiting New Players

For a regular poker game to remain vital, new players should be brought in from time to time. How many and how often should be a group decision, but regardless, recruitment should be discussed. Certain criteria should be agreed upon. Some Friday Night Poker Clubs are limited to professional men—no women and no average pedestrians. Some groups are strictly for women. Some groups are only for members of a sports team, such as a community softball team.

To keep the game flowing peacefully, some thought must be given to the personality of the group and of the individual players. Finding like-minded people is sometimes difficult, and one bad apple can spoil the whole barrel. I was in a Friday Night Poker Club, and one of the guys brought in a lady who was determined to change our rules. In the second week, she arrived early and started harassing each person as they walked in the door. She didn't like our limits, our choice of games, our deadline to quit, the food or cigar smoke. We had a problem. The next day, the regulars decided she should not be asked to come back, which was a difficult decision because she was a wild and loose player with a lot of money to lose. But we still made the choice to exclude her because we felt the game was worth saving and felt she would be a negative factor for us in the long run. After this event, we were more careful who we invited. Our present policy is to have a probation period. A new recruit must be invited and continue to be invited at least five times before he or she becomes a regular.

Playing Too Many Wild Games—Sometimes a newcomer to the game is overpowered by playing too many weird games. When a new player comes into the game, it is usually a wise move to stick to more conventional poker games. Let them learn the unconventional games one at a time. Space out the exotic games until the person gets comfortable. Remember, you need new blood and money to keep the game robust. Be a bit considerate. The best assurance of longevity for your poker game is to have a strong waiting list. Don't run off new players with too many wild games.

Cheating

Again, I devote a chapter to cheating later on, but I feel the need to mention it here as well. Cheating can destroy a good Friday Night Poker Group.

Most of the cheating done at this level is amateurish and easy to detect if you know what to look for. It often consists of peeking at the next card, *culling* (a crude attempt to stack the deck), deck switching and sometimes collusion between two players.

The biggest problem happens when a cheat is discovered. Suppose one of the regulars is detected cheating. What do you do? Kick him out of the game? When you think about it, cheating is a terrible issue to have to deal with. It has many implications.

My suggestion is to give the cheater one warning, making it clear that more than one person is aware of the cheating and that there will be only one warning. Then it will be exclusion from the game. Do not discuss the problem with anyone outside the game. If the person is detected cheating again, take definitive action. If one person is allowed to cheat, others will start. Clear and precise action is called for.

FRIDAY NIGHT STRATEGY

I've already covered strategy in the section prior to this one; now let's apply some of it to the types of hands and players you're likely to come across in a Friday Night Poker Club or apartment game. These types of games are the first venue where you can really apply what you've learned on the use of position, patience, planning and emotional control. These skills will apply to whatever poker game you are in, from the kitchen table to the exotic casinos in London, Monaco, Crete, Las Vegas or Atlantic City.

So let's talk about some specific ideas and tactics that will help you win in a Friday Night or apartment game, which are different from casino games. One important difference is the choice of games available. Poker games in a casino are usually confined to one game like $3–$6 Texas Hold 'Em or $4–$8 Seven-Card Stud. The casino determines what game is to be played at each table. You either play that game or you don't play. On very few occasions, a casino game is played that will allow any flop game to be played: Omaha Hold 'Em, Texas Hold 'Em, Pineapple Hold 'Em or any of these games straight high or high/low. Or they will allow any stud game to be played: Seven-Card Stud, Five-Card Stud, Seven-Card Stud, High/Low Split, etc.

A home game or a Friday Night Game usually allows any and all games, some straight, some wild. Because of the variety of games allowed, you can develop some strategies that will give you just a few percentage points' advantage over your opponents. Although this seems like an insignificant amount, over the course of a year a slight advantage could reap substantial monetary rewards. You'll also discover a whole new way of observing the game and the players. A little bit here, a big chunk there and you will astonish yourself how much you will be able to scrutinize and add to your advantages.

I wish I could tell you how much (in dollars) each strategy is worth in percentages over your opponents. I can't do that because I don't know the sophistication of your opponents. They might have little knowledge of the game or they could be very, very good. In fact, consider that you might be "the fish." As one poker writer put it, "Look around the table and ask yourself which one is the biggest sucker. If you don't know, it might be you."

Button or Random Games

One strategy to beware of that will give you a small advantage in your game, if it allows different kinds of games, is never, never sit to the immediate left of a person who always or usually calls a *button game*. A button game is a game like draw poker or any of the flop games, in which the person to the immediate left of the dealer is first to act. A random position game is a game like stud where the first person to act is determined by the cards that are showing. Either the person with the highest or lowest card is first to act. Therefore, position is usually changing. Everyone has an equal chance to act first or last. No one will know who will be first to act until after the next card is dealt. If others are forced to act before you, you will make much better decisions. As you learned in the chapter on position, you are in a horrible position when you are the first to act. Once every round, you will be forced to act first for the entire hand in a button game.

If the person to your right always or usually calls a button game, you will be the most vulnerable for that hand. If the person to your right always or usually calls a random position game, your chances of acting first are the same as anyone else. I make it a point to know what game each player likes to call. When I arrive at the game, I sit to the left of a player who likes to play stud or some other random position game. This gives me a small edge.

Of course, when it is your deal, it is just elementary that you will usually call a game that will give you the advantage of acting last, a button game. Then you are in the driver's seat and will be last to act for that hand. Everyone will act before you have to commit yourself. You will find that sometimes a bet will win the small pot, even when you have nothing.

If you have doubts about this strategy, I ask you to test it out. Find out for yourself how it works. I know that you will be a believer before long.

Don't Become a Rock

One important fact comes across as we progress with our poker learning. That fact is—conservative play is usually a winner. I am not talking about timid play. A timid player is afraid to bet, even when he or she thinks they have the best hand. A good poker player is conservative, yet aggressive. Be conservative in your hand selection, but aggressive when you have a good hand. Keep that conservative/aggressive concept in your mind and develop it. That concept is a winner.

The downside of conservative play in a home game or a Friday Night Poker Club is that you will be labeled a "rock" by the other players. When that happens, they may drop out of the game when you play. A warning bell will go off in their heads when you enter the action. They will evaluate their cards more critically and drop out at the first chance. That will cost you money. They will not call those good hands you have waited for all night. When you have been labeled a "rock," your profits will drop.

The way to avoid the label of "rock" is to selectively enter the action with marginal hands. Let me put a lot of emphasis on that word "selectively." I give that advice with extreme caution, because you must be acutely aware of position before you play any marginal hand. Since position has some power, you *must* have that power working for you to compensate for playing a marginal hand. A marginal hand is not a solid moneymaker, so you must assure yourself of having something going for you.

When you play a marginal hand occasionally and happen to win the pot or show your hand, it is certainly good to call attention to your hand. Suppose you played this hand in Texas Hold 'Em from late position, preferably last position:

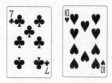

The flop came:

It would be appropriate to call attention to your seven-ten off-suit. Maybe you could say something like "I love to flop two pairs" or "Seven-ten off-suit is one of my favorite hands." When you point out that you also play trash, you are doing a couple of things:

1. You are giving others the impression that you are a loose player.
2. You are telling them it is okay to also play trash.

Either of those messages will certainly help keep you from being labeled "The Rock."

Getting the "rock" label in a public casino or card room is not nearly so bad. The turnover of players is much, much higher, and your style of play won't be known to as many players. But even if the label is placed on you there, you should take some corrective action by playing a few hands loose so you won't be so predictable.

TRANSITION FROM KITCHEN TABLE TO CASINO

Where do we cut our poker teeth? I did it with my buddies in high school. Like most folks, we couldn't remember if a flush beat a straight or how to figure one full house over another. All we had was a deck of old cards, some matchsticks and desire—the desire to compete.

What is this "compete" stuff? Are most humans born with the drive to compete, or is it a product of environment? Maybe the scientific fellows can answer that; I sure can't. What I do know is I have it, and the people I play poker with and baseball with and basketball with also have it. We play to compete. We call it fun, but that fun usually is better fun when we win, right?

I looked up the word "compete" in *Webster's*. It said:

> To strive consciously or unconsciously for an objective (as position, profit or a prize): be in a state of rivalry

That tells it like it is: "to strive." We young guys at that poker table back on the farm in Minnesota would strive, alright. You would think a world championship was on the line. We manipulated, we tried to bluff, we did some crazy stuff, "striving" to win the pot of matchsticks. And we didn't have a cent to gain. It was all just for the glory of being the winner! Somewhere be-

tween the heart and the soul is this "compete" thing that
drives us to extend ourselves to win. For us guys sitting at the
kitchen table on a very cold winter night with the wind howling
and the snow blowing outside, we strove to be the winner. All
four of us had the same urge to outdo the others. We each used
our very best mental powers to win more matchsticks than anyone else. Whatever that drive is, the striving to win is what pro-
pels every poker game I've ever seen. And I love it.

IS THERE A NATURAL PROGRESSION?

Yes, I believe there is. For most people, not all. A friend of
mine, Carl, played his first hand of poker in a college dormi-
tory. He said the game was going almost continuously, twenty-
four hours a day. Most of the players who were regulars had
participated in poker games with their families. So poker in
college was a natural progression for them. The ladies and
gentlemen whom I play with tell stories with a common
thread. They started playing as young people, playing with
family and friends. Slowly, they explored the more sophisti-
cated options of Friday night groups and card rooms. They
were all a bit afraid at first as they ventured out. Some fell by
the wayside. The ones I've met are the ones who became comfortable and found that poker in public card rooms has many
advantages, and so they have continued to play. For most,
poker is recreation. For some, poker has become a challenge,
a mountain to climb, a skill to acquire.

WHAT IS A NATURAL PROGRESSION FOR YOU?

The first question to answer is, Do you want to progress? I assume you want to become a better poker player because you are
reading this book, but do you want to progress past your kitchen
table, past the family games to Friday night poker games with a

regular bunch of people? If you play poker one night a month or one night a week, do you want to find a situation where you play either more often or with different people? If you have aspirations to expand your poker horizons, this section is for you. If you do not feel the craving to move beyond your present poker level, this section is just plain information. There is absolutely nothing wrong with wanting to stay where you are. Certainly not everyone wants to become a regular at a casino or a card room. I have found there is a sort of subculture of regular poker players in each community all across the country. Every city and country has a group or groups of people who play poker regularly. You can join one of these groups if you want. My caution would be to do your homework first. The cost of taking poker lessons from those guys could be high.

A LITTLE BIT OF KNOWLEDGE

Poker is strange in one respect. Have you noticed that when someone has played a little bit of poker, they feel they really understand the game? I see it all the time, and it makes me a lot of money. Trust me when I tell you that a little bit of knowledge is a dangerous thing in poker. Now I am talking *real* dangerous. Maybe people think poker is like roulette, where once you learn how to play, you just play it. The ball comes up red or black with a number. In roulette you either win or lose. Perhaps they believe there is no strategy to poker. A whole bunch of people consider poker to be all luck, so they can just play and not worry about skill. Poker is a tough game. Repeat: Poker is a tough game. If you know more about correct strategies than the other guy, you are giving Lady Luck a break. She is the kind of gal that will visit you as often as anyone else, and if you help her out a bit, she will begin to come around more often.

Now, let's go back to expanding your poker environment. If you have not been exposed to the card room or casino atmosphere, you need more information.

12

THE CARD CLUB & CASINO SCENE

WHEN YOU FIRST WALK INTO one of the really big California card clubs, called Freeway Poker Houses, you will see literally hundreds of table games in progress. It is quite a sight, and it can be intimidating. The first time I walked into one, I was afraid to sit down at the table. I could only stand and watch. The action was so fast and so smooth, it was hard to follow. The dealer read the hands and passed the pot, the winner tossed him a tip while he shuffled the cards and the next hand was under way. No clumsy shuffling and dealing by your buddy. No waiting for someone to return from getting a cup of coffee. The game in a card room or casino is fast and furious.

The players also appear to be so indifferent. Sometimes new players are greeted with impatience, even rudeness. If you should need more time to study your hand or call a raise, often someone will make a derogatory comment. Since the dealer makes most of his money from tips, he, of course, wants the game to move along. For good reason, a novice is often intimidated. I will say that in games I have seen, for the most part, the seasoned veterans welcome a new player to the game. After all, they see the new player as a pigeon to be plucked, a fish to be gutted.

Registration

The first thing you have to do in most card clubs is register with the person running the player board. That board shows all the games in progress. You usually have a choice of several games and several limits. You may be able to play $3–$6 Texas Hold 'Em, $4–$8 Texas Hold 'Em, $6–$12 Texas Hold 'Em, $2–$4 Seven-Card Stud, etc. As you look at the board, notice that the person taking names only uses the players' initials.

If you should want to play the higher-limit games, usually you will be referred to another area and another person will take your initials for the game of your choice. Most of the time there is a waiting list. That list moves fast because when they get enough players for a game, they open a new table.

The Staff

In any good-size poker room, there are a number of staff people responsible for keeping the games going on. First of all is the *dealer*. He or she is in the box (dealing) for about half an hour and then moves to another table. These dealers get a break every couple of hours or so depending on the number of games and the number of dealers. Then there is someone called the *brush*. He or she takes care of several tables, calling out seat openings and making sure the players get what they need, like cocktails or coffee. Then there are the *chip runners*. They either carry chips with them or they will go to the cage to get chips for you. Finally there are the *floorpersons*. Depending on how many tables are open in a section, there can be one or two floorpersons. These people will keep the games moving, directing players to their seats, opening or combining tables, arranging for table changes and solving disputes that might arise. The dealers usually answer most questions, but sometimes a controversy comes up. The dealer simply calls the floorperson over and explains what happened, and the floorperson makes the decision on what to do.

These are the significant players you will find in a major card room. They are all there to make you comfortable and assist you in playing poker. Obviously, they are employed by the card room or casino, and it is in their best interest to keep the games going smoothly and to make them last as long as possible. They are also there to protect you from anyone who has the desire to cheat.

Also, don't be afraid to ask these people questions, no matter how stupid you think they are. They have a vested interest in making sure that you enjoy your game and keep coming back to play. Therefore, they are usually all too willing to answer any question. If possible, it is best to ask your questions when you are taking a break or before you sit down to play. The other players may not take kindly to being interrupted.

13

TABLE COURTESY & CUSTOMS

WHEN YOUR INITIALS ARE CALLED for the Seven-Card Stud game, you will be escorted to a table by a brush person. The chip runner will take your money, announcing the amount you have coming to the dealer, and disappear with your money. Before you can think about that, the next hand is dealt and you are caught up in the game.

You look at your hole cards and your first up card:

A player with the four of clubs showing is forced to start the betting. He bets $1. You tell the dealer that you call even though you don't have your chips yet. The dealer relays the message to the other players that you have called. Five players call the opening wager. The next card is dealt. Your card is the queen of hearts.

Hmmmm. You have a pair of jacks and three cards to a straight, three cards to a flush and three cards to a straight flush, which is not a bad hand. However, the dealer has pointed to a man who has a pair of kings showing, including the king of hearts. He has the high hand and must be the first to act. He can either check or bet. He bets $3. Two people call his wager. The dealer now points to you. It is time to act. You hesitate, pondering what to do. The dealer again points to you. A player across the table says something gruff that you don't quite hear, but it is obviously not a compliment, because you are holding up the game. In frustration, you turn your cards over and give them to the dealer.

Frustrated or not, you made the correct decision. You folded a hand that had potential but was beaten in sight. The frustration only contributed to your hesitancy. The action is very fast, and the other players are not always courteous. In fact, a number of them are downright rude.

TABLE STAKES

Most poker games are played with the simple rule of table stakes. That means you can only play with the money in front of you. You cannot, as some movies portray, go into your pocket for more cash or borrow money from a friend. Only the money you put on the table can be used.

Rat Holing

It is against the rules and ethics of poker to *remove* cash or chips from the table. I have seen this done many, many times. The reason for the rule is the understanding that if you remove money from the table, the other players will not have the opportunity to win that money back. You won it from them; they should have the right to try to win it back. Taking money off the table is called *rat holing*.

Sidepots

Discussing table stakes brings up another occurrence, that of "going all in" or the resulting "side pots." Suppose you start playing a hand and you have $20 in front of you. The pot is raised and re-raised and you end up with only $1 when you have to call a bet of $5. What happens now? Because you do not have the necessary funds to call the full bet and you cannot go into your pocket to get more money, do you have to forfeit the pot? No. What happens is the creation of a side pot. Suppose there are a total of four players at the point where you have the $1 and the bet is $5. One dollar is taken from the bet of each player (including your $1) and placed in the "main pot." Then the remaining four dollars from the other three players is placed in a side pot for a total of $12. You are required to do no further betting and so you watch the rest of the hand. You are dealt in for all remaining cards. However, you can only win the main pot, not the side pot because you have not contributed to that.

This rule is in effect because it protects you. If you lose the pot it is because of your cards, not because you ran out of money. Sometimes more than one side pot is created as other players run out of money on the table. Figuring the side pots can be a bit tricky, so it is a good idea for you to think about how to do it if you play in a pass-the-deal game. When you have a center dealer, the dealer does all the figuring. That is what he or she is paid to do. Dealers will also make mistakes, so try to get up to speed on how a side pot is figured. It could save you money.

COPING WITH RUDE PLAYERS

As the game goes on, you start hearing more things the players say to each other. Some of them are acquainted and make derogatory statements to each other. Some of them are pretty rough statements. Since you have come from games that are slower and where all the people know each other, you are a bit shocked at the rudeness. Players seem to be attacking each other.

I truly believe in the statement, "Poker is fun." It sure doesn't seem like fun to me to talk disparagingly about someone else. You will hear it, but I hope you will not get caught up in it. Poker is supposed to be entertaining, and it can be so if you just ignore these guys who are angry or resentful or out of control or whatever. Maybe they are big losers or maybe they just have negative personalities.

There are a couple of coping mechanisms I use. One, I try to totally ignore them. If one of them says something negative to me, I just smile and continue to play my own game. Second, if the talk gets too much for me, I simply ask for a table change. One thing I promise myself never to do is to get angry with them. I try hard to blank them out. I have come to play poker and have a good time.

DON'T GET OVERCONFIDENT

Although it is easy to become intimidated when you first play with the big boys, a few big wins can quickly help you gain confidence—perhaps too much. Although it is vital to be confident when you play in order to project competence and intimidate the other players, you must be careful not to get too cocky. When you start playing with serious, experienced players, the people who really know the odds, the players who have seen guys like you come and go and who know how to manipulate you, that overconfidence will lead to your downfall. Be keenly aware that the more you learn, the more there is to learn. Believing you are one of the best players in a casino is a trap that will drain your finances quickly.

HOUSE RULES

Regardless of where you play in the world, there are "house rules." Because there are various ways to play poker and the practices differ from place to place, certain house rules have been adopted. This is true for casinos and card rooms, for apartment games, and for kitchen-table games with only family members playing. In the bigger card rooms, the house rules are usually posted on the wall in a prominent place. In apartment games the rules are usually talked about as the game gets started (or written down, as I suggested previously). In home games, the rules are a bit more informal, because the game is usually a social event between friends and family.

The typical rules state what kind of deck is used. Does it have a Joker (usually called the Bug), and if so, how is it to be used? Another rule can be about what kind of game or games will be played. Some allow for only one type of game to be played for the duration of a session, like Five-Card Draw. Others allow certain types of games, like all stud games with no wild cards. Others allow only flop games. Some allow dealer's choice, where any kind of straight poker game or a game with any number of wild cards is possible.

One house rule you should determine immediately is if check-raising is allowed. Check-raising is outlawed in many private games because some consider it unsportsmanlike. Make sure you know if you can do it; otherwise you could offend the other players. Most casinos and cards rooms allow check-raising, but again, find out as soon as possible.

In local games, also ask about any customs that you might not be familiar with. Usually your asking will be honored and appreciated. I played in a card room in California that did not allow deck changes. It was only after I had asked for a deck change that I found out the local custom.

Be on the lookout for other house rules like the use of *shills* and *props*. A shill is an employee of the card room who plays with the money the house gives him. These are usually good players who are employed to help keep the game going. Props are proposition players who play with their own money and usually work for an hourly wage. They also are there to help keep the game going. The props are also good players who supplement their poker income with wages. Usually the dealer will identify any shill or prop that is in your game.

COMMON TABLE COURTESY & PROCEDURES

You will find some procedures quite different from the typical home games. Here are a few examples and hints on how to get along and avoid being the target of embarrassing or sarcastic remarks.

Don't "Splash" the Pot—In the home games I have been involved in, the players simply toss their chips into the pot. If you do that more than once in a card room, you will probably be reprimanded. The correct procedure is to place your chips in front of you, several inches from your cards. This way the center dealer will be able to count your chips to be sure you have not put in too few or too many. Also, this assists the dealer in making sure the pot is correct when there are several raises and/or an all-in wager.

Placing the chips neatly stacked will help keep the game moving along smoothly.

Don't Make Your Own Change—A huge no-no is to make your own change from the pot. The dealer and the other players will speak sharply to you if you touch any chips in the center. Making change is the center dealer's job. Let him do it and save yourself some embarrassment.

Don't Grab the Pot—When you win, suppress your glee and the urge to sweep the pot into your lap. Do not reach for the chips until the center dealer has pushed the pot to you. I have seen players stand up with a grand gesture and try to scoop all the chips. Again, you will be reprimanded. Those chips are not yours until the dealer indicates they are.

Raise Boldly and Clearly—If you wish to make a raise, it is a good habit to announce "raise" in a clear, strong voice. Card rooms have a rule against "string bets," and if you announce your intentions, you will have no problems. Suppose you have to call a bet of $10 and want to make a raise of $10. If you grab a handful of chips and don't announce a raise, and you do not have enough chips in your hand to complete the raise, the dealer will not allow you to move back to your stack to get more chips *unless* you announce a raise. The reason for this rule is that some sharpies have taken advantage of novice players and will watch an opponent carefully while they take the chips out to the betting zone. If they get a certain reaction, they will then attempt to raise. They will not be allowed to do that by the house rules. This is for the protection of the average player.

Protect Your Cards—Always protect your cards with either a chip or some object like a good luck piece. I haven't seen it often, but some players will try to foul your hand by shoving their discards into your cards. If you do not have the hand protected, your hand will be declared dead. Another danger of having your hand unprotected is that the dealer might sweep your cards unintentionally. Again, your cards are dead. Protect them.

Act in Turn—An important ethic of the game of poker is acting in turn. If you know you are going to fold your hand, wait until the player or players in front of you have acted before you discard or even indicate that you will discard. For instance, if I am playing on your right and you are the last to act, and I know that you are going to fold, I might decide to call the last bet. If I did not know what you were going to do, I would have thrown my cards away. It is a courtesy of the game to always act in turn.

You will also find some cute players who will deliberately make a move out of turn like saying, "I raise." They know that the raise is not enforceable because it was done out of turn. When the action gets to them, they simply check. They do this on the chance they can get a free card.

Table Stakes—Most card room regulations call for table stakes. That means that you cannot go into your pocket for more money during a hand. Between hands and before you look at your cards, you can get more money from your pocket. You can also tell the dealer you are intending to bring out more cash by saying something like, "I am playing X number of dollars back." I always keep enough chips on the table or, if cash is allowed on the table, I keep some extra cash right under my chips. Don't worry about the cash being stolen. All of the better casinos and card rooms have cameras on the tables at all times.

Ask for Time—As a courtesy to the other players and the dealer, ask for time if you need a few seconds to analyze the play. If you ask for time, the other players are usually accommodating.

Posting a Blind—Many card rooms have the rule that when you first sit down, you must post an amount equivalent to the big blind. If the open seat where you are seated is just a hand or two in front of the blinds, ask to wait until the blind gets to your position. Then you won't have to pay the blind twice in a couple of hands. This is not a big item, but a way to save a bet or two.

14

THE CONSTANT CHANGE OF PLAYERS

CASINO AND CARD ROOM PLAY is dramatically different from a home game, a Friday night game with a regular bunch or even an apartment game with an occasional new player. The home game, in most cases, has the usual lineup. So in the home game you can get a real good understanding of how they all approach the game of poker. Uncle George is wild and crazy, Grandpa is slow and conservative. Whatever the mix, you soon have a feel for how each person plays because you have seen them all.

Sometimes one of the Friday night guys will change styles somewhat, but most of us don't change all that often or all that much. We are all victims of habit. Once we learn those habits, you can immediately notice any significant change in style. Occasionally, a new player is brought into the game by one of the regulars. This calls for an evaluation of the style of poker this new player has. Does this person know the rules of your game? Is he or she a real good player? Is he or she, perhaps, a novice and a pigeon? What is his or her style and what are their tendencies? Is he or she a fun person to have in the game?

READING PLAYERS

When you move into the card room setting, the situation changes very fast. Players come and go, changing tables frequently. Sometimes a player will experience a tough beat, grab his chips and leave without a word to anyone. He just departs in a hurry. It is not at all uncommon, if you should go for a cup of coffee, that half the table could change and there would be different players by the time you get back. This kind of player traffic simply calls for new and better adapting techniques.

Essentially, coping with all these players coming and going means you must make some general reads as quickly as possible. That means you focus on the new player immediately and put him in broad categories. Suppose a new lady sits down and seems very much at home with the dealer, brush and floorperson. She greets one or more of the players at the table. Obviously, this is not her first time in that card room. All this tells you is that she is not a total novice. The second thing you notice is how she handles her chips. Does she sit down and start manipulating them or rolling them with her fingers? Does she put the chips in the pot with confidence and a smooth action or does she falter in handling them? The fact that she can handle chips with ease does not mean she can play a lick, but it tells you she is not a new player at the poker table.

Next, watch her eyes. Is she observing the action of the other players, or is she only conscious of what hand she has? If she is carefully watching the other players, this is a clue that she could be a very good player. If she is only concerned about her own cards and is constantly looking back at her hole cards, she might be a weaker player.

The Best Clue

As soon as she plays a hand, notice what she turns over. At this point you have your best clue. You immediately replay the hand in your head. What was her position when she called or raised? That information gives you a strong indication as to how well she plays position. If she played rag cards in early or early middle position, she is not a strong player. If she called or raised into a chancy situation, like another player having an obvious flush or flush draw, she is telling you she plays with little regard for her bankroll. By far the best clue you get about her is how well she played the hand. You find that out by replaying the hand from her perspective.

Another general clue to look for is how many hands she plays. Some players come to play, and they will play no matter what. If she is one of those, you have a "fish" in the game, so bait your hook. Does she stay until the end, hoping to draw a miracle card to a weak hand? If the game is Seven-Card Stud, does she stay with a low pair all the way to seventh street hoping to catch trips? In Texas Hold 'Em, does she play that low pair in the hole all the way to the end, again hoping to make a set? These are strong indications that this lady is most welcome at your table.

The Strong Player

The clues that a strong player gives are much different from the lady I just described. He or she will usually sit quietly for several hands, seldom moving except to watch the other players. His eyes will see everything. He will handle his chips with ease and self-possession. Everything he does will be poised. He will play just a few times each round, and when he turns over a hand, it will usually win the pot. Again, if you see his hand, replay it in your head. This will give you the most important clue. Does he play position well? Does he raise in appropriate situations? How did he react to someone else's raise or re-raise? When you see a player like this enter the game, you know a solid player is now in the game. This is the first general category in which you can place the new player. Since this player might only be at the table for a short time, it is meaningful to get a fix on him before you battle him for the pot.

If the player is a weak player, proceed with lesser hands. If the player is a strong player, proceed with only very good hands.

As soon as you have assessed this player, fine-tune the evaluation. Keep in mind that you will be fooled occasionally. The weak-appearing player might be putting on an act. He or she might be trying to seem frail and be really setting a trap. As each hand unfolds, you will be able to refine your initial assessment. Also, the person who appears at first to be a strong player can fool you. It could be that he or she has learned to be observant when they first enter the game. They will sit quietly for a while because they have read how important it is to observe other players. However, after a brief period, they cannot resist the action and plunge in on almost every hand.

Starting Hand Clues

Another important clue to a new player's capability is the choice he makes in starting hands. Quantity and quality are the way you judge that. If he plays a lot of hands, you can start to downgrade his play. It is simply impossible for a person to play a lot of hands and be a consistent winner. Sure, he might win big on any given session, but his overall win record will be terrible. Quantity is a very accurate measure of a person's ability to play the game of poker.

It is also quite possible for a person to sit down at the table and get a big run of good cards. Then he will play almost every hand but you won't be able to determine if he is playing trash or if he is on a good run unless you see his hands. So you also have to look at the quality of his hand selection. If he is playing a lot and turns over the winner time after time, he is likely to be on a good run. When he turns over his hands and the hands are consistently good, even if he is playing a lot, you must withhold judgment until you see more of his play.

A good run of cards seldom lasts very long. Watch carefully and check out the quality along with the quantity.

One sure sign of a good player is patience. That means he will play only quality cards. Quality cards are usually quite scarce. If the new player appears to be patiently waiting for a good starting hand, he is interested in quality, not quantity. So when the new player is throwing away a lot of hands early on, you have a good player in the game. In addition, if his judgment of quality is good, beware. You have a top-notch player as a competitor.

TOURNAMENT PLAY

Tournaments are held all over the country now, in many sizes, varieties, and forms. In my view, tournaments are opportunities to:

- get valuable experience at a reasonable cost
- test out some new ideas
- put some jingle in your jeans

Let's take a look at the experience opportunity. For the recreational player or the novice, tournament play can put a limit on how much you invest at any given time. The beginning player is just going to have to pay a price to learn this game. If he or she gets lucky along the way, hopefully that price will not be terribly high. You will learn in the next chapter that tournament play is quite different from live action or ring games. However, tournaments will provide you ample opportunities to observe how people react, how usual and unusual betting situations happen, and the value of certain hands in various circumstances. Since the cost of playing a small tournament is usually small, the experience is worth the money.

Testing out new ideas? It has been my experience that the more concepts and tactics I learn about poker, the more I am exposed to other concepts and tactics. Isn't that true of a lot of things? The more you know about something, the more you find out there is to know. Tournament play is structured in such a way that you can explore new strategies without spending a bundle. Tournaments truly offer a base to test ideas, a possibility of winning some cash and a chance to learn how the game ought to be played at a reasonable price.

Jingle in the jeans? Since a tournament is held in a short period of time, luck becomes a moderate factor. Anyone can get lucky. In fact, expect to get lucky. If you happen to get lucky at just the right time, you can easily win a tournament and turn a small investment into quite a return. That win can easily pay for many other tournament entry fees. So in that sense, some of your education is paid for.

15

TOURNAMENT STRUCTURE & STRATEGIES

THERE ARE MANY, MANY tournament structures. I will describe a common one to give you an idea of what a real tournament is like. This is an actual tournament that I play in on a regular basis. Different communities and card rooms have different structures.

This tournament is limited to four tables of Texas Hold 'Em. It is a structured tournament with a $35 buy-in, for which you get $600 in tournament chips. Thirty dollars of that buy-in goes into the prize money pool, $5 goes to the house.

At any time, a player can purchase another $600 in tournament chips, this time for $30. After three twenty-minute rounds, there is a break, at which time a player can purchase a double re-buy of $1200 for $30. After the break there are no more re-buys. This tournament has a limit of two re-buys.

The first three rounds of play are limit play, starting with blinds of $10 and $20 and betting limits of $20 and $40. After twenty minutes the blinds go up to $15 and $30 and the betting limits are $30 and $60. After twenty minutes more the blinds go up to $25 and $50 and the betting is $50 and $100. We play twenty minutes at this level and then have the break. After the break, the tournament becomes no-limit with the blinds doubling every twenty minutes. This is an elimination tournament, so as the players run out of chips and leave the game, the tables are combined to have an equal number of players at each table. When the number of active players is reduced to ten, action is stopped and the ten players draw for seats at the final table. The blinds are now quite high and the action tense. This is the best time for tournament addicts like me.

This tournament pays four places, with first place getting 40% of the prize pool, second getting 30%, third getting 20% and fourth 10%.

RULES FOR THE WORLD SERIES OF POKER

To help you to understand how tournaments work, I've included the rules set up by Binion's Horseshoe in Las Vegas for the World Series of Poker. They are as follows:

Any person 21 years of age or over is eligible to enter any and all tournament events by posting the required buy-in and entry fee before the start of each event. Play for each event will begin at a predetermined hour and continue until a winner is declared. Exceptions are multi-day events. There will be a 10-minute break every two hours and a one-hour dinner break. Each event is a normal freeze-out, with the game continuing until one player has all the chips. Players may not acquire additional chips beyond the original buy-in except in re-buy tournaments. Limits and blinds will be raised at regularly scheduled intervals. Players are eliminated from the tournament when they lose their chips. Tables will be systematically combined as players are eliminated. The last remaining player at the final table will be declared the winner of that event. The entry fee pays for table time. There will be no additional charge.

FOR EACH EVENT:

1. Participants are wagering on their ability to remain in the competition until the conclusion.

2. The house is not a party to any wager and will only serve to oversee the event and the wagers made among participants. All monies distributed will be from the fund collected from the participants at the start of the event.

3. The house retains the right to cancel or alter any event.

TOURNAMENT STRATEGIES

Elimination tournaments have been around for centuries. Remember the Forum in Rome? Recently, casinos and card rooms have discovered that poker tournaments are lucrative. The tournament by itself does not bring in a lot of cash for the card room, but the side action and the increased traffic is a bonanza. A tournament brings customers in the door. Most of them play in the tournament, which has a small "entry fee." Most of those players wash out of the competition quite quickly and join the regular ring games that are available. The regular ring games are where the card room makes its money. It is a good deal for them and a very, very good deal for the recreational player. When you factor in an occasional win, you will find that tournaments will accelerate the learning process for a bargain figure.

I must add a disclaimer to the above claim of accelerated learning process for a bargain price: While you get a bargain at the tournament table, you must change your style of play. Tournament play is much different from regular play. Most of the poker players you will encounter are not aware of that. Consequently, they play tournament poker the same way they play ring games. That is a mistake.

When you win a pot in a ring game, you win chips that can be exchanged for real coin of the realm. Each and every chip is worth real spendable cash. Not so in a tournament. All you win in a tournament is a bunch of chips called, appropriately enough, tournament chips. They have no value outside the tournament. The only use for those tournament chips is to try to get more of them until you have them all. An elimination tournament is played down to the last person. When one person has ALL the chips, he wins. Therefore, the payoff is appallingly top-heavy. Those early wins at the table don't mean a thing unless you finish at or near the top. The only winners are the very last players. In very big tournaments where there are hundreds of competitors, they will often pay down to the 27th player. Paying to the 18th place is more usual. The person who finishes 27th or 18th might get his buy-in plus a pittance. In smaller tournaments the payoff is usually the top three players, with the number one player getting more than the other two combined. That is why you must get to the top. Otherwise you get nothing or, at best, very little.

Basically, what you want to do is make it to the final table with enough chips to win the tournament. If you are just barely surviving and get to the final table with just a few chips, you have to get very, very lucky to win. Good play at the final table has more to do with the power of betting courage and chips than it has to do with card power. If you don't have enough chips to intimidate, you will be intimidated. In order to win your share of the tournaments you must have some firepower at that final table.

Early Hand Selection

With very few exceptions, in the early rounds of a Texas Hold 'Em tournament, I play only two hands: a pair of aces and a pair of kings. In the early rounds, I do not try to trap with those hands. If the hand is raised in front of me and I have one of these hands, I will re-raise. My goal is to get heads-up with the first raiser. That is pretty simple and straightforward. What about the exceptions, like a pair of queens? The pair of ladies is still a good hand, and I will play it in certain situations. If I should get them in an early or early middle position, sometimes I will raise with them. My goal in raising with the queens is to see who calls my raise. Since this is early, I seldom know very much about my opponents. Therefore, I am most cautious. If a player I know to be conservative calls, I know I must catch an excellent flop. A flop like this is a good flop for those ladies:

or maybe even:

Since I have an overpair, I will lead bet. My biggest fear is running into a player with a pair of jacks in his hand or any other player who has made a set. However, since that is quite rare, I will bet until someone raises.

Flops I will seldom bet at are:

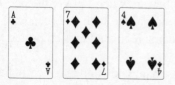

or:

or

In my opinion, that pair of queens can become a liability on those flops. The people who called my raise must have something. With either the ace or the king out there, the chance that I have a losing hand is too big. I want to conserve my chips and not burn them off in dangerous situations. If someone bets, I will usually fold. My goal is to get to the last three players, and burning up chips is not the way to do it. I will wait for better opportunities.

Other times, playing that pair of queens from early or early middle position, I will just call with them. My goal in calling is to catch someone stealing or to hit a big flop. I will do this maybe ten to fifteen percent of the time I catch those queens in early or early middle position. What I am doing is sending a message to the other players that they should beware when I am in the pot. If I don't catch a good flop, I am simply done with the queens. If I catch a good flop, I can do some damage to another's chips and to his or her emotions.

When I catch the pair of queens in late position and the pot has not been raised, I will usually raise. This gives the impression I am trying to steal the blinds. Again, unless I catch a favorable flop, I will simply not invest any chips. Once in a great while, I might bet once to see what happens and to prevent someone trying to steal the pot on the turn.

If I catch queens in late position and it is raised in front of me, I throw my hand away.

Draw Hands—One important example of how you must change your style of play is that in a tournament, you should not play draw hands until you get to the final table(s). In early play, you simply cannot afford the luxury of playing drawing hands that might or might not win. Go only with the very big suited cards or the big pairs. Do not call with suited connectors like:

or

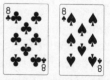

Although these cards look mighty good, resist the temptation to play them. Remember the payoff is big but ONLY if you make the last two or three players. You just cannot afford to lose in the early rounds. Wait for those powerful hands. At the early stages the blinds or antes are not that big, so plan to play only the very best of cards. What about playing these hands?

In the past, I have played these hands early on in the tournament. Never again. Against competition, they are drawing hands. You must improve to win. Chances of improvement are too great and not worth the risk, in my opinion. I wouldn't even play an ace-king or king-queen early on.

Middle Round Hand Selection

You are now in the middle of the tournament, still going strong. The blinds have now gone up a few times. The weak and unlucky are starting to be weeded out. My hand selection begins to change slightly. By now, the other players at the table have noticed that I muck almost every hand and I generally do not defend my blinds. That table image now becomes important. The observant players will put me in the rock or conservative category. That is exactly what I want them to do.

I now also have a fix on what some of the other players are doing in a tournament setting. Some have lost most of their chips and are just praying for a good hand before they are blinded out. Some have been up and down, winning several pots and losing several. Some players have been very lucky and have lots of chips.

I am watching closely how each of these players is reacting to their particular circumstance.

Since most of the players at my table will be respecting a raise that I might make, I can now loosen up in certain situations. In order to make the final table with at least my share of chips, I must use this middle time for chip gathering. If the pot has not been raised, in late or late middle position, I will put in a raise with any two suited picture cards (I include the ace as a picture card). Blind stealing is important for chip gathering, but at this point I will seldom make a raise with a nothing hand, or what is called a pure steal. Suppose, in an unraised pot, I have this hand on the button:

That one picture card is enough to raise with against the blinds, especially if they have a moderate stack of chips that they want to conserve. Remember, I have the table image of being a very tight player.

If one person has called when the action reaches me in late position and I have this hand:

I will raise. My reasoning is that I have two things going for me. That person has told me by his call that he doesn't have a premium hand. Unless he hits his hand on the flop he will check to me. It will be quite difficult for him to call my bet because he has no idea what I might have. I don't have to hit my hand to bet. Therefore I have the power of position going for me, plus I have a decent hand that I might hit. The middle time in a tournament is chip accumulation time. Again, the goal is to reach the final table with chip power. If I wash out at this level, then so be it. This is the gamble I feel I must take to become part of the bigger payoff.

Final Table Hand Selection

Let's suppose I have been fortunate in the fall of the cards and have made it to the final table with the average number of chips. What is my strategy for hand selection at this point?

Hand selection in the early stages has been vitally important. At the middle level, it became slightly less important because I started to gamble more. Now, hand selection becomes even less important at the final table. Surprised?

Let's review the emotional state of the players who have also reached the final table. They all know that as each player is eliminated, their payoff increases. Most players become very conservative. Most players almost freeze up at the final table. They are willing to blind away much of their stack in the hopes that others will engage in mortal combat.

Now is the time to be bold, to risk. Now is the time to take advantage of their timidness. Depending on position and the activity ahead of you, any middle or big pair deserves a raise. Sometimes I will try to set a trap with a big pair like kings or aces. Any big or even middle suited connectors deserves a raise. With a hand like:

Go ahead and raise if the pot has not already been raised. I will even re-raise with this hand if I feel the situation is right. For instance, a re-raise is appropriate if I can put the person who made the first raise all in. I also want to force everyone else to call a double raise. Calling a double raise will be tough to do, and if it happens it will tell me that I am up against a powerful hand. By putting the raiser all in, I stand a good chance of eliminating a player and moving me that much closer to the final three. Eliminating players is the goal of everyone in the tournament. If my mother were in the tournament, I would try to force her out.

Now is the time to attack the people with the small stacks. Don't be afraid of putting them all in if you have a decent hand. It is also the time to withdraw from the action if two or more competitors decide to contest the pot. Even if you have a very good hand, like K♥-Q♥, give it up. Let them fight it out. One will lose a lot of chips and become a cripple that you can pick off later.

Test Every Hand

As stated, you must survive the early rounds to get to the money-winning final hand. Therefore, every hand should be subject to a survival test. Will the hand take you out of the tournament if you play it? Are you willing to risk first-place money on this hand?

Say you are in early position and you look at this hand in the second round in a Texas Hold 'Em tournament:

That is a good-looking hand, right? So ask yourself, "Am I willing to risk first-place money on this hand?" If you say no, I will be proud. If you say yes, please come and play where I play.

In a tournament, that A♣-Q♠ is trash except at the final table and possibly during chip gathering. You cannot afford to play A♣-Q♠ in the early part of a tournament. *Every* hand must be examined with an eye on the final three places. Otherwise, you will become part of that 80% to 90% of the players who end up with no dollars.

Please notice I am emphasizing the dollar return. This is but one of the many advantages you get from tournaments. Suppose you play that A♣-Q♠ and get thrashed by an ace-king. That becomes a hands-on lesson you will never forget.

Now let's suppose you are in a Seven-Card Stud tournament and you raise with this hand:

One opponent calls your raise with a queen showing. On the next card you catch the 7♣ and he catches the Q♦. He has the high hand on board and so he is first to act and he bets. What should you do? You had the best hand at the beginning. The other person has paired his door card and is either running a very good bluff, has two pairs or three queens. Fold those aces and wait for the next opportunity. Do not pour chips down this hole. It is time to hit the survival button.

Get Out Early

One other important technique for survival that is often overlooked is not throwing good chips into the pot trying to rescue chips you have already deposited. Staying to see one more card can be a fatal flaw in tournament play. Maybe you have made a good raise with a solid hand, caught a bit of the flop and now have a marginal draw that could win you the pot. Say you played this hand:

and the flop came:

One person has stayed in and bets into you. What should you do? First, analyze the situation. What do you have that could make you a winner? The other person probably has a queen or he might have king-jack or nine-jack for a straight draw. It is possible he has queen-ten, which gives him two pairs. He probably does not have three queens or three tens, since he likely would have raised before the flop with either a pair of tens or a pair of queens.

What to do? You have two overcards that could allow you to win the pot if they should come. However, either one of them could also make the opponent a straight. You also have an inside straight draw, a longshot draw for the nuts if the board does not pair and no flush possibilities come up. You also have a back-door flush draw for the nuts, if the board does not pair. My thoughts are that the situation is rather chancy and not worth investing any more money. You started with a good hand but did not catch a good flop, and the opponent probably has a better hand or a better draw. In my opinion, it is time to concede and get on to the next case.

Defending the Blinds

Attacking the blinds is the equivalent of trying to steal the blind money in the pot. Since the blinds are a forced wager and are placed before the player is dealt the cards, quite often the blinds have weak hands. The theory behind attacking the blinds is that the chances are high they have weak cards *and* they are in very bad position. (Stealing the antes in an ante game is somewhat similar.) Attacking the blinds is a big part of tournament play. Therefore, knowing when to defend a blind is an important skill. Make no mistake, defending the blinds is a tough job. When in a blind that is under attack, most of your decisions should be based on your evaluation of the person who is raising to drive you out and, of course, the strength of your cards.

Small Blind—Seldom is the small blind worth defending. If I should catch a pair of jacks or above, I will defend the small blind against one raiser in late position.

Sometimes, if I should catch the pair of aces or kings, I will reraise with those bigger pairs; other times I will try to trap. In the early and middle rounds of a tournament, I will not defend with any kind of a draw hand.

During the rounds at the final table when I catch a decent hand, I might try a bluff or a semi-bluff, depending on my chip status, the chip status of the raiser and his or her personality and my assessment of their emotional state. Another tactic is a check-raise from the small blind. This move can win some checks.

Big Blind—Protecting the big blind is somewhat different. The small blind always has to act before the big blind, and that adds to the problems of a small blind. When the blinds are attacked and the small blind folds, I will seldom defend a big blind during the early and middle rounds unless the circumstances are just right. The major problem is the horrible position. The blinds have to act first, and unless you get substantial help on the flop, it is usually a waste of chips to defend. Unless I catch the big pairs, in the interest of survival, I often concede the pot.

I am cognizant that the other players will soon become aware that I do not defend blinds and will raise with trash. That's okay during early and middle play. That is just part of the table image I want to convey. When the last table play begins, I am a turncoat. My style is different. Now I will defend with decent hands and try to trap. This role reversal is important for the final table, when most players are tenuous and timid. If I catch them in a steal, I will want them to respect my play and fold when I raise. It is all part of a plan to outplay them and win the tournament.

IMPORTANT POKER CONCEPTS

This book is for the player who is serious about becoming a winning poker player. Therefore, I have added some important material that is a part of successful play. These chapters are about good money management, cheating, good books, videos and computer software. There is also a cautionary chapter on gambling addiction.

16

MONEY MANAGEMENT

IF YOU WANT SOME EXCITEMENT in your life, ask a couple of poker players about the true meaning of money management. If you were to conduct a poll of 100 poker players and poker writers about money management, you would get widely divergent responses. Why? A very good question. Few poker concepts have taken on such disparate meanings. A clear definition is elusive.

Some years ago the double-M word, money management, got a lot of ink. Let me quote Mike Caro, "The Mad Genius" of poker, from his excellent book, *Fundamental Secrets of Poker*:

> *"To me, back then, money management had become a detested term, misunderstood and misused. To most of those who bandied the double-M term about it meant some kind of magic salvation from losing."*

If you are looking in this chapter for the "true" meaning of poker money management, you will be disappointed. I truly believe that most of the distinctly different definitions are mostly true. I believe each knowledgeable person has a valid definition, at least a definition that is meaningful to him or her. It just is a wonderful phenomenon that there can be so many good definitions.

KNOWING WHEN TO QUIT

Some players and some poker writers will say that money management is knowing when to quit a game. These players and writers will tell us that the time to quit a game is when certain monetary goals are met. Once the player gets, say, $130 ahead, he or she should quit for the day. Quit, even if you have played ten minutes. Maybe it will take you eight hours or twelve hours to reach the goal, but you stay until you either get too tired or too broke or you make the goal. I guess you could say that their definition of money management is setting and meeting a goal.

Another group of players and poker writers would say almost the opposite. It would be their contention that a player should not have a goal, but to play as long as certain conditions were met. Winning or losing in any one session would not be a consideration and would not be one of the conditions. These people are saying the player should play as long as:

- the game is good, meaning the player would be at least among the best players at the table
- the player is not tired
- the player is not experiencing any personal or emotional distress

This group of players and poker writers would say that a loss is not a reason to quit a game as long as the above conditions are met. If a loss causes the player to tilt or become emotionally distressed, then he should quit. They would define the game of poker as being one very long session, starting with the very first hand ever dealt to the person and ending with the last hand dealt to him. That concept has merit in my opinion.

PLAYING WITH SHORT MONEY

Most experienced poker players would agree that part of the definition of money management should include advice against playing with money that should be used for essentials like food, rent and utilities. These players are experienced enough to know that when one risks the money slotted for basics, one's mental attitude is such that they are almost sure to lose the money. When one plays under that kind of pressure, experience has shown the player will usually lose. Somehow the distress of playing with short money sets up a mental or emotional block that will affect your play.

Another aspect of playing with short money is playing at limits too rich for the bankroll. Comfort level seems to have a direct connection with being able to win. For instance, you can absolutely dominate a game of $4–$8 Seven-Card Stud. If you have a bankroll of $1,000, you may be comfortable at that level. However, if you were to take that same bankroll to a $10–$20 game or a $15–$30 game, you are most likely to change your style of play and probably would not win. The $1,000 bankroll is simply not big enough to be comfortable in the bigger games. At some level in your consciousness, you feel the pressure and somehow it changes your game. Please remember, this is not just my opinion, but the consensus among the good and great players who validate this concept. Please be forewarned to be prepared with a bigger bankroll when you move up in limits. Play within your comfort zone until you have set aside the safety net to be able to endure a couple of sizable losses.

Instinct is so terribly important in the process of winning at poker. If your instinct tells you to make a certain play and then you question that thought because of your weak money, even your hesitation has probably given away your strategy. Playing on desperation money is bad business. You need to have decent operating capital, just like any other business.

PICK YOUR GAME WISELY

Another definition of money management is choosing a game. Some games just don't provide the win possibilities of others. If you see an open seat in a game of mostly very solid players who only have a small amount of money on the table, ask yourself if you really want to invest your time and money in a game where your winnings are very limited and losses unlimited. If that is the only game in town, you might choose to play. Otherwise, look around for better pickings. If you should lose big in that kind of game, the chances are the good players will pick up their chips and leave. You won't have the chance to get back to even. Good money management is choosing wisely where to invest your time and money.

DON'T RAID YOUR BANKROLL

Everyone does it. I have done it. You will too. When that bankroll becomes strong, you can think of some luxuries to buy. You rationalize that you have been playing well and will continue to play well. Therefore, that bankroll will go nowhere but up. Wrong! There is only one exception: when you start with, say, a bankroll of $1,000 and you are successful. You move up to the $15–$30 game and continue to do well. If you do well enough to get $40,000 or $50,000 in that bankroll AND there is no possibility of you playing at any higher limits, you can safely take the top 10% for luxuries.

Look at it this way: When you started with that $1,000, you were undercapitalized. You played well or got lucky and built the precious bankroll up to where it should be. But you will get a long run of bad cards. Let me say it again with more emphasis. **YOU WILL GET A LONG RUN OF BAD CARDS.**

Unless you have the bankroll and the emotional stability to withstand that long run, those bad cards will destroy your poker playing career. Believe me, I have seen it many, many times. Players come into the game and do well for a while. They study the game, the books, the videos, the software. They win money for a year, two years, five years. Then you see them on the rail wearing their gold chains and Rolex watch, watching the action. They try to borrow money. Later you see them without the Rolex and the gold chains, still trying to borrow money. Then you don't see them anymore. What happened? Bad cards. Bad cards that caused bad or desperate play. I am suggesting that if those players had carefully guarded their big bankrolls when they had them, they would have been able to withstand that long run of bad cards. Protect that bankroll. Life and cards are fickle. Be prepared for the drought. I can promise you, that drought will come.

KEEP GOOD RECORDS

One bit of advice to help you manage your money is to keep accurate records of your wins and losses in various games. There are very few players who are equally good at all games. It is usual for a person to develop a preference for one or two games. For instance, I prefer Texas Hold 'Em. Because I like Texas Hold 'Em, I have become more proficient at it, which is reflected in my records.

These records of your wins and losses also give you information. If I need a valid reason for wanting to play Texas Hold 'Em, all I have to do is look at my records. That proves I win more times at Hold 'Em than I do at Seven-Card Stud or Omaha Hold 'Em. I also notice that I win more often in Seven-Card Stud with deuces wild than I do with some other wild games. I can't give a definitive answer as to why at this moment, but information is the point of keeping records.

Some of the information you should record is your win rate per hour of play; which games are the most profitable; the value of tournament play compared to regular ring games. When you have the correct data in front of you, you make better choices. Should you play more tournaments or fewer tournaments? Should you stick to the game you like to play or would it be more profitable to play a different game? Do you make more money before midnight or after? This kind of information will give you a slight edge over your competition, and at the same time help you manage your money by determining which games are more profitable for you. The good player is always looking for ways to increase his edge, no matter how minor.

Try to remember that it is important that you record, in detail, the losses as well as the wins. Look especially hard at why you lost. When you have several big losses in a row, it is time to take a serious look at your game. Do you have some leaks? Are you going on tilt? Are you planning enough? The basic question is, "Is it me or is it the cards?" If it is you, you need to take corrective action. That is the information you get from keeping good records. The extra effort will pay off in the long run.

17

GAMBLING ADDICTION

AN ADDICTION TO GAMBLING is a VERY serious problem, and money is not the only thing at stake. You could also lose your dignity, family, friends and loved ones. Addiction to gambling makes life a living hell. I know, because I have seen a few victims and done some extensive reading on the subject.

I once knew a man who became addicted to gambling in general. He started out playing poker, but moved on to blackjack and craps. Poker, being a game of skill, did not provide him with the feedback he needed to continue his addiction. This man had a small business started by his father. He therefore could take a lot of time off to sustain his addiction. He ended up falsifying his company books and selling many personal possessions. His wife left him, and his health failed. He once was a man in charge of his life, well liked by all. He became a gambling bum. He didn't shave, bathe or change clothes. He just hung out with people who were gamblers. One day, when he was about halfway down, I saw him bring in his son's coin collection to try to sell so he could get money to gamble. That is a true story about how addiction destroyed a person, a family man who, from all appearances, was a happy individual.

Perhaps you are questioning your own attitude toward gambling. There is a big difference between avid enthusiasm and addiction. Here are some symptoms to help you decide if you have crossed the line between the two. Do you:

- constantly make an effort to quit gambling, but seldom are able to abstain for any length of time?
- make an effort to conceal your gambling activities from family and friends?
- have a feeling of being driven by a force that you cannot control?
- never allow yourself to leave the game with a win, unless the game breaks?
- have a nagging feeling of remorse because you gamble?
- have a compulsion to gamble when you should be at a family function?

If you or someone you know exhibits two or more of these symptoms, my advice is to get professional help and contact Gambler's Anonymous. As with Alcoholics Anonymous, GA people are in recovery and are extremely helpful to anyone with a possible problem. They have answers you don't even have questions for yet. They have walked all the miles you have walked, experienced the utter degradation of loss of self, and can give you a hand up if you need it. It is very important to note that this addiction is almost always impossible to solve by yourself. Very, very few people can overcome this alone.

If you do not have a Gamblers Anonymous chapter in your area, write to Gamblers Anonymous, P.O. Box 17173, Los Angeles, CA 90017.

18

CHEATING

As I'VE PREVIOUSLY MENTIONED, poker is a game of deception. Lying, manipulation and duplicity are actions that are approved of and even admired in a poker game as long as they are done within the constraints of the rules. Cheating breaks these rules in a deliberate attempt to win at the game, which, because there is money involved, makes the offense far worse. Why endanger your winnings with a bit of swindling?

The main reason not to cheat is the destruction it causes to your reputation. I am constantly puzzled why most cheaters do not seem to think through the consequences if they are caught. If one is found cheating in a family game for pennies or matches or toothpicks, there is some shame and perhaps discipline involved. If one is caught cheating in a Friday Night Poker Club, he or she will probably be excluded and embarrassed in front of friends. Wouldn't that be neat? If your group is made up of members of your softball team, everyone would know you were caught cheating. It would be worse if the group consisted of colleagues from work. If the cheater is detected in a casino, the police might be called and the person may be prosecuted. The least that will happen is that he or she will be barred for life from the casino.

MECHANICS

I have known a few dealers who were *mechanics* (someone good enough to deal themselves or someone else a winning hand). However, the percentage of cheating dealers is very small; the majority are honest and deal straight up, especially in a casino or card room. If they are caught in a casino, their careers are in great jeopardy. The casinos also have them under constant surveillance.

A good mechanic is almost impossible to detect stacking the deck. They are smooth and seem so casual. In private, they have shown me some unbelievable stuff. Very little is sleight of hand. Most manipulation of the deck is just a matter of locating the cards and keeping them in the correct order.

The mechanic who chooses to become a crook usually works with an accomplice. The dealer waits for the opportune moment and deals one or more customers good hands. He deals his accomplice a better hand. They have a set of signals so the accomplice knows when this is happening. Most of the time the accomplice will sit in the first or last seat so the communications are easy.

If you suspect a scam at the table you are at, I suggest you leave the game immediately and remain out until that dealer's shift is over. Get the name of the dealer and the accomplice, if possible. Later make a phone call to the casino manager. Do not call the floorperson or the poker room manager. It is very unlikely either of them is involved, but it has happened. The casino manager will follow up on your complaint. In the interest of justice, do not discuss your suspicions with anyone else until the casino manager has had time to investigate. You could be wrong and you would do damage to the reputation of an innocent person. Ask the manager to call you back with an update of his investigation. No doubt, security will focus their cameras on that dealer and he will be watched closely for any indications of dishonesty. Remember, the casino has a big vested interest in staying squeaky clean. Those folks are your best allies.

Palming Chips—If you suspect a dealer of palming chips and placing them in his tip pocket or jar, here is a technique that works. The dealer who steals has the problem of getting that chip into his pocket or tip jar without being seen. He or she will usually wait until the person who won the pot tosses him or her a tip. Then the dealer will drop the chips into the jar together.

A way to detect a dealer who palms is to wait until you win a pot, then wait to tip the dealer until he is shuffling the cards. Few people are able to hold a stolen chip in their hands while shuffling.

If you should get evidence that a dealer is palming chips, follow the same procedure of phoning the casino manager.

PARTNERS

A far more common occurrence at the poker table is two people playing partners. Their method of operation is to have signals set up so when one of them gets a big hand, the other will raise or re-raise to get more money in the pot. During the last betting round the partner with the poor hand will throw his cards away. By then they have gotten money from one or more innocent people.

When you suspect partners, watch to see if you can detect the signals. That is an important piece of information. You can then either defeat them at their game or you can tell the floorman. It is extremely unlikely the floorman is in on that kind of scam, and the floorman will want these guys out of his room.

APARTMENT GAMES

The apartment game is where your greatest danger lies. The cheater can slip into the game and perhaps be known to only one or two of the regulars. After he makes his hit, you won't see him anymore. Marked cards are possible, but the most likely thing for him or her to do is to hold out cards.

Hold Out Artists

A hold out artist will have something on the table like a napkin and slip a card or two under that object. When this player gets an ace, he will slip it underneath. The hold out artist is also capable of slipping a card off the table. When the right combination comes along, he will substitute cards and show you the winner.

One way to counter this move is to change decks occasionally. Be sure to have a different colored deck, and it is best to have at least four colors available.

I feel the best thing to do if you should spot a hold out con is just leave. Some of those guys are crazy and carry a gun! If you spot something funny, change decks. If it still looks suspicious, get out of there.

The usual cheaters in apartment games are quite clumsy. That doesn't make them any less dangerous. If they are stupid enough to try to cheat, they might be stupid enough to violate people. The best protection is to simply find another game.

19

RESEARCH

I WOULD BE REMISS IF I DID NOT encourage you to research poker further. There is an endless selection of literature, videos and computer software on the subject of poker. Like almost everything else, some of these materials are excellent, some are average and some are mediocre. I am presenting here what I consider to be the best of the current material. Please regard this as my opinion only. I am offering this information because these items have helped me. I have reviewed almost all literature, videos and computer software that are currently on the market. These are my recommendations, in no specific order of importance or quality. If any of these items interest you, I recommend that you write to the publisher and ask for a current price list and any other material they have for sale.

POKER EXPERTS

Brunson, Doyle

Doyle Brunson is a two-time World Champion as determined in the World Series of Poker played at Binion's Horseshoe Casino in April and May every year. He has written and compiled what many refer to as "The Bible" of poker, *SUPER/SYSTEM, A Course in Power Poker.*

SUPER/SYSTEM is published by B & G Publishing Co., Inc., Las Vegas, NV 89102. Mr. Brunson, acting as both writer and editor, has asked what he considers the finest group of players to play the game to write about various games of poker. Mike Caro, "The Mad Genius of Poker," wrote the chapter on draw poker; Joey Hawthorne wrote the section on lowball poker, including Ace-to-Five, Deuce-to-Seven and Razz; David Reese composed the chapter on Seven-Card Stud; David Sklansky wrote about Seven-Card Stud, High/Split; Bobby Baldwin, another World Champion, wrote the section on Limit Texas Hold 'Em; and Mr. Brunson wrote about his specialty, No-limit Texas Hold 'Em.

This tome was first published in 1979 under the title *How I Made Over $1,000,000 Playing Poker.* This will be a timeless book that is certainly worth the $50 price tag. Each section provides authoritative information gleaned from countless hours of research at the table, over endless cups of coffee comparing notes with other experts and hours at the computer. Seldom has a book on any subject been written by people with this kind of expertise. What is unique is the card-by-card analysis of strategy and advice. There is also an excellent comprehensive glossary. The last section is an incredible statistics segment compiled by Mike Caro.

According to Doyle is another Brunson book consisting of a compilation of magazine articles. They provide insight into everyday encounters at the poker table. This book might be difficult to find. Try the gaming bookstores in Las Vegas and other places.

Caro, Mike

What else can I say about Mike Caro except that he is the guru of poker writers and poker players? His writing is authoritative because he is bright, is experienced in most poker circles, and thoroughly researches his material. I give a blanket approval on all his writings, videos, and computer software.

The Body Language of Poker is a new edition of the classic book, *Book of Tells*. *The Body Language of Poker* was first published in 1984. Mr. Caro captures in pictures the tells that can save you a tremendous amount of money. Included with each tell is a reliability factor for weak, average and strong players. Mr. Caro gives Value Per Hour classification for each tell based on the dollar limit of the game.

Examples of tells: *Caro's Law of Tells, #24: Beware of sighs and sounds of sorrow. Caro's Law of Tells, #19: A forceful or exaggerated bet usually means weakness.*

This book is quality. If you plan to develop poker skills, get this book from any of the gambling bookstores. Published by MGI, 4535 West Sahara, Suite 105, Las Vegas, NV 89102.

Fundamental Secrets of Poker, ISBN 1-880069-00-8. Published in 1991 by MGI, 4535 West Sahara, Suite 105, Las Vegas, NV 89102. Like all of Mike Caro's information, this book is high quality. His first chapter is titled "Why You Really Can Beat Poker". The material is highlighted with powerful concepts that have been proven. For example, "In the long run; in poker, you don't get paid to win pots—you get paid to make the right decisions." Mr. Caro gives advice on the popular games of Seven-Card Stud and Texas Hold 'Em as well as money management, psychology and tournament tips.

Mr. Caro offers a potpourri of other material besides these books. His software is reviewed in the software section that follows. Contact Mr. Caro at the MGI address listed above for a list of materials available.

Elias, George "Profit"

Awesome Profits. This 380-page book covers some popular home games and most of the currently popular games like Razz, Texas Hold 'Em, Seven-Card Stud, Seven-Card Stud High/Low

Split, Omaha, Lowball, etc. Mr. Elias is a down home type of person who has a lot of fun playing and writing about playing. I cannot help but like this guy. The author gives practical strategies for regular games and tournament play and a lot of other information on playing in casinos and card rooms. This book can be ordered from Ace Hi Publishing, 2250 E. Tropicana Avenue, 19-478, Las Vegas, NV 89119.

Jones, Lee

Winning Low Limit Hold 'Em. This is an excellent book for the recreational player and newcomer to Texas Hold 'Em. Perhaps this is the best book available for the beginner who wants to quickly learn Texas Hold 'Em. After a section to explain the technical aspects of Hold 'Em, the author gives vital information of how to play "From Deal to Showdown." The beauty of the book is found in the definitive actions that should normally be taken before and after the flop. Suppose you play A-K. This book will give you ideas on how to play if you flop the top pair, two pairs, straight and flush draws, etc. After each section is a neat little quiz on the material to help solidify the point the author is making.

I believe this to be the most pragmatic book available for Texas Hold 'Em. It is available from ConJelCo, 132 Radcliff Drive, Pittsburgh, PA 15237. When writing, also request a catalog of other gaming products they stock.

Percy, George

Seven-Card Stud, The Waiting Game. My copy of the book has a copyright date of 1979, and it has since been reissued at $8.95. This is a compact book that gets right to the heart of Seven-Card Stud. If you follow Mr. Percy's advice, you will win. He doesn't spend a lot of time on poker philosophy, but he does tell you how to win at Seven-Card Stud. The way to win is quite simple—you wait. You can order the book from Mr. Percy directly at 6679 Five Penny Circle, Las Vegas, NV 89120, or from gaming bookstores.

Sklansky, David

No listing of poker books would be complete without David Sklansky's books. He is a scholar of the highest order. His poker writings are superior. A resident of Las Vegas, where the best poker players in the world either live or visit, he plays against the toughest competition in the world.

Hold 'Em Poker. In this book, Mr. Sklansky does a top notch job of introducing Texas Hold 'Em. After the introduction he gets right to the basics of position and hand selection and devotes the greater share of the book to strategy. Another good section is on probabilities. There is a very small glossary and an index.

Theory of Poker. Formerly titled *Winning Poker* and before that *Poker Theory,* this book is not for the beginner. It has real depth and needs to be digested like a college textbook. Mr. Sklansky has created a superb piece of work and what I consider a must-read for any serious player.

Sklansky on Poker. Another quality production and a must-read for ardent players.

Getting the Best of It. This book appears to be a compilation of articles published in another form. Good reading, but on diverse subjects.

TOURNAMENT BOOKS

The popularity explosion of tournament play has created a new specialization within the poker community. Some very good ring game players have developed distinctive techniques just for tournament play. Because only the last players get paid in a freeze-out tournament, unique tactics combined with standard solid play have been developed. Most of this new information was closely

192 / ANDY NELSON

guarded by the good players. Now a couple of tournament champions have chosen to write about the stratagems they have developed. I have reviewed one of the best books.

The Secret to Winning Big in Tournament Poker, by Ken Buntjer.

I like this book. Mr. Buntjer is a dedicated tournament player. He even hints that tournament play is for REAL poker players, and ring games are for beginners and those less capable of authentic competition. He calls himself a "Major Tournament Specialist." Certainly he has some winning credentials to back up this claim.

What I like about his book is the way he presents practical help and how he breaks up a tournament into twelve steps. In each of the twelve steps he gives specific information on how each one should be played in order that the player can progress with sufficient chips to get to the final two or three players. Mr. Buntjer writes about the all-important player identification factors, the variations of personalities and what patterns to look for, breaking them down into seven stereotypes. Then he makes definite recommendations on how to play against each of the seven player stereotypes in various situations. This is very useful information to have, as is the information on how to play against two opponents and then against one opponent. He also gives advice on tipping and what to do when the tournament is over. While this book is pricey ($49.95) it is worth the money to a serious tournament player. Order from Poker Productions, Inc., P.O. Box 55427, Portland, OR 97238. Poker Productions produces videos as well as books, so ask for a catalog of their latest publications.

Tom McEvoy, World Champion in 1983, wrote the first quality book on tournament play. The book went out of print but has been expanded and reissued by Poker Plus Publishing, 4535 West Sahara, Suite 105, Las Vegas, NV 89102. It is priced at $39.95, and I have heard this is a quality book. The new title is *Tournament Poker.*

COMPUTER SOFTWARE

Much has been said and written about the pluses and minuses of the computer as a poker research tool. Many argue the computer is virtually useless because humans play poker and react to the changing actions and reactions of other humans. There is absolutely no question that humans are different from computers. Computers and humans do not have the same operating systems. Are we then to discount computers completely? By no means. Computers offer us wonderful capabilities to do serious research.

Poker Probe

Mike Caro has developed an incredible research tool called *Poker Probe*. It runs on IBM compatibles with modest hardware requirements. The program offers fifteen games or variations of games including Draw, Texas Hold 'Em, Omaha, Stud, and others. Mr. Caro has built in qualifiers so split games with the "8 or better" can be researched.

Poker Probe is not designed to simulate an actual poker game. In *Probe*, no one folds. All hands are dealt randomly and each hand is played to the end. Some say this is a weakness. I say it is a strength because this kind of research tells me the horsepower of each hand that I test in comparison to every other hand. I can easily and quickly run a test of a million hands of a particular starting hand. Let's say I want to know what percent of the time a hand like Q♥-Q♦ 7♦ will win in Seven-Card Stud. That will tell me how often I can expect that pair of queens to hold up.

Just for fun, let's run that pair of queens with the seven kicker and see what we can expect from it. I ran that exact pair of queens with the seven of diamonds. I programmed it to run one million hands, and it tested at 896,147 hands per hour.

What did I discover? That pair of queens wins an average of 24.57% of the time. This was against six opponents who each had an approximate win rate of 12.59%. The queens won 245,682 of the million hands. In those win hands were 53 straight flushes, 5,332 four-of-a-kinds, 70,958 full houses, 25,181 flushes, 5,050 straights, 47,594 three-of-a-kinds, 82,600 two pairs. In the loss column, there were no losses for the straight flushes that this hand caught, 19 losses when it made four-of-a-kind, 4,990 losses for full houses, 8,284 losses for flushes, 2,824 losses for straights, 50,484 losses for three-of-a-kinds, and 327,143 losses for two pairs.

What can I conclude from this one run? Many things. One, when I make two pairs, queens up, I lose a lot. Two, when I make three-of-a-kind, I lose more than I win. My best chances are when I make a full house, and a flush isn't bad either. The straight horsepower of a pair of queens with a seven kicker to match one of the queens in suit is almost 25%. In a real game, I would raise with that pair of queens to try to reduce the field. When I am able to do that, my win rate will go up sharply.

Let's compare that situation. Suppose I raise and get called by three opponents. What is my win rate now? *Poker Probe* says that instead of 245,682 wins, I have recorded 421,686 wins against three opponents. These three opponents played all the way to the end, taking all seven cards. In a live action game, no doubt some of them would have folded. However, in order for them to call a raise, one could assume they had a bit better hands than a random sample. One has to allow for those factors. The win rate on the second trial was 42.17% as compared to 24.57%. Dramatically different. Are computer runs like this useful? I believe they are.

One other feature of *Poker Probe* is a prediction game that is challenging. Choosing Seven-Card Stud, Razz, Texas Hold 'Em or Omaha, the player gets to predict the number of times certain randomly dealt hands will win in one hundred tries. I have learned a lot from the prediction game. *Poker Probe* is available on both 5.25" and 3.5" disks from Mad Genius Software, 4535 West Sahara, Suite 105, Las Vegas, NV 89102.

Wilson Software

From the computer software that I have reviewed, it is my opinion that Wilson Software of South Lake Tahoe has quality products. They just blew me away with their *Turbo Texas Hold 'Em* game. I wrote to tell them that I didn't consider their latest version an upgrade, but a revolution. It is marvelous.

The game is just jammed full of features. It runs on IBM compatibles and has both DOS and Windows applications. You can program each and every player at the table. You can use the players the company has designed or you can make up your own players. You set the limits, rake, maximum raises, etc. And you can "zip to the end" whenever you decide to fold, thus speeding up the game.

This program also does fantastic research. You program in when players call, raise or drop, and you can find out how much a pair of sevens is worth in a test of say a million hands. The *Hand Analyzer* is also a powerful tool. It gives you advice on what to do with any situation, the odds on winning and a dollar valuation of what that hand is worth if played many times. These evaluations are all based on what the limits are, the structure of the blinds, the number of raises, the position of the button and the aggressiveness or looseness of the game.

Wilson Software has a number of other really great software packages. Their Omaha High/Low Split program is also a very strong product. The player can modify the playing styles of each of the players up to ten or he can create completely new players to come into the game. Betting limits can be set, the number of raises controlled, the structure of the blinds changed at will, the position of the button and the aggressiveness/passiveness adjusted.

The point count system is outstanding. The player can choose from a number of systems built in or he can create his own. Because of the complexity of choosing a starting hand in Omaha, point systems really help a player evaluate the two-card combinations he is holding. This powerful and useful feature is called the *Omaha High-Low Split Hand Analyzer*.

Wilson Software has three other products on the market at this writing, *Turbo Seven-Card Stud, Turbo Omaha High* and a *Turbo Texas Hold 'Em Tournament* that can control the number of players from 10 to 320. Mr. Wilson has confirmed that his company is also working on tournament versions of Omaha and Seven-Card Stud. Write to Wilson Software, P.O. Box 612674, South Lake Tahoe, CA 96152, for a complete list of products and prices.

Amarillo Slim Dealer's Choice

This is another software package that I like. It has some nice features that make it fun to play. It has 28 poker variations in one package. It is simple to operate and works on IBM compatible computers. It is available from Villa Crespo Software, 1725 McGovern Street, Highland Park, IL 50035.

POKER VIDEOS

The latest arrivals on the poker instructional scene are videos. I have reviewed several and I like three of them. The first two reviewed here were produced and narrated by Ben Tracy.

How to Beat Winning Hold 'Em Players

It is obvious after viewing this tape that Mr. Tracy is an excellent Hold 'Em player. And he is an excellent video producer. He gives solid information from beginning to end, starting with the statement, "Hold 'Em is more than a card game, it is a mind game."

Yes, the man knows his poker. He gives *practical* advice and illustrates this advice with poker hands that make the point perfectly clear. He is also empathetic with the stresses and effort necessary to succeed at Texas Hold 'Em. I like his "Law of GWID." That is "Getting What I Deserve" when we stray from a solid approach to the game.

Mr. Tracy delves into "The Seven Deadly Hold 'Em Traps" and then "Ten Commandments for Winning." This tape is not aimed at the novice player but is trying to upgrade that novice player to the intermediate level. If you are in this category, this video will return handsome benefits.

Sklansky, The Video

The other video that is of high quality and produced by Ben Tracy features one of the premier players of poker, David Sklansky, who also happens to have written some excellent books. Some claim Mr. Sklansky has had more impact on the game of poker than any other world-class player.

The video begins with excerpts from a rare poker seminar given by Mr. Sklansky. This is where he says, "I'm trying to tell you things that the typical player doesn't know." The setting for the video is Binion's Horseshoe Casino in Las Vegas during the twenty-fifth anniversary of the World Series of Poker. Mr. Tracy includes vignette interviews with notable players who comment on the contribution to poker made by Mr. Sklansky. This is an excellent video for the player who is serious about learning the game of poker. These videos are available from Poker Productions, Inc., P.O. Box 55427, Portland, OR 97238. Write for current prices and a catalog of products. Mr. Tracy would also appreciate a personal note explaining where you are in your poker career.

Poker for All

Mr. Steve Fox, President of the National Poker Association—a nonprofit corporation dedicated to the advancement of poker as legal entertainment—produced this excellent video. Mr. Fox presents basic information about poker in a clear and precise manner. This is an excellent video for the person who is first learning poker or is moving from home games to a casino/card room setting. This video will be quite helpful in the transition to the confusion of the bigger card rooms.

Mr. Fox defines several poker terms and rules, like how side pots are determined, and the differences between antes, blinds and forced bets. He also explains the courtesies and customs of poker and briefly describes the three families of poker: draw poker, stud poker and the Hold 'Em games.

This video can be ordered from The National Poker Association, 2460 Juniper Ave., Boulder, CO 80304. It is a bargain for the beginner and recreational player.

GLOSSARY

Aces Up: Two pairs, one of which is a pair of aces. A♦-A♣-7♠-7♥-4♦ is an example.

Active Player: A player still involved in the pot, who still has his hand and is competing for the money.

All Blue: A flush of either clubs or spades. An example: K♠-7♣-2♣-Q♠-8♠

All Pink: A flush of either diamonds or hearts.

Ante: Money placed in the pot before the cards are dealt. Each player must post the same amount of money or chips. See also *Blind*.

Baby: A small card, usually a five or lower. When the ace is used as either a high or low card (in games like lowball and certain high/low split games), it is also considered a baby card.

Back Door: When a player makes a hand he wasn't drawing for, it is called "back dooring." Suppose a player starts out hoping for a straight and catches enough cards of one suit to make a flush. Or he could start out drawing for a flush and by accident make a straight.

Back-raise: A re-raise. Suppose player A makes a bet. Player B raises. When the action gets back to player A, he re-raises. That is a back-raise.

Bad Beat: When a big hand is beaten by someone who draws to a long-shot or a low-percentage hand and makes it. If there is only one card in the deck that will make an opponent's hand a winner, that is a very low-percentage draw. If the opponent catches that card, that is called a bad beat.

Belly-buster Straight Draw: Another name for the infamous inside straight draw. If you should have the hand 7♣-5♥-9♣-8♦, a six of any suit would make a straight. Only four cards will complete the straight. The inside or belly-buster straight draw is contrasted to the open-end straight draw in a hand such as 7♥-6♦-9♠-8♥. In the open-end straight draw, eight cards (any five or any ten in this case) will complete the straight.

Betting Unit: In a limit game of poker the game is defined by the amount you can bet. For instance, a $3–$6 game tells us we can bet $3 in the first betting round and $6 in the later betting rounds. Each bet is a unit. If the initial bet has been raised twice before the action gets to you, you must call three units.

Bicycle: The lowest possible hand in lowball such as A♥-2♦-3♣-4♠-5♦. Even though the bicycle is a straight, the straight is disregarded in games like California Lowball.

Big Blind: The second (sometimes the third) blind bet. Regardless of how many blinds are placed, the "Big Blind" is always the largest of the required blinds. (See also *Live Blinds*.)

Big Dog: A hand that is the underdog. When two or more hands are competing for the pot, one hand is the favorite and one hand is the "dog" or "underdog." The underdog has the lowest percentage chance to win.

Big Full: The best full house in a hand where more than one full house is made. The hand J♥-J♦-J♣-7♥-7♣ is the "Big Full" over the "Underfull" of 9♥-9♦-9♠-5♦-5♣.

Big Slick: The ace-king in any combination of suits in Texas Hold 'Em.

Blank: A card that is not of value to a player's hand. For instance, if a person has four hearts in his hand and is hoping to catch another heart to make a flush but instead catches a spade that has no other value, that is a "blank" card.

Blind: A blind is comparable to the ante; that is money placed in the pot before the cards are dealt. Blinds are usually placed to the left of the dealer button.

Blinded Out: This is a term often used in tournament play where a person has not caught cards good enough to compete and consequently all his chips are used up paying the blinds. Tournaments have progressive blinds which often double every twenty minutes to two hours. In that way a lot of a player's chips are blinded away and he is out of the tournament.

Bluff: An attempt to win the pot by betting without having what the player considers a winning hand. He or she is hoping the other person will fold, thus conceding the pot.

Board: Any cards that are placed face up during a game. These can be individual cards as in Seven-Card Stud and Five-Card Stud or they could be community cards as in Texas Hold 'Em and Omaha Hold 'Em.

Boxed Card: A card in the deck that faces the wrong way. When the dealer begins to shuffle the deck, occasionally one or more cards are collected that face the wrong way.

BR: A term that refers to bankroll. Keeping the bankroll of any active poker player is absolutely crucial.

Broadway: An ace-high straight, such as A♥-K♣-Q♦-J♣-T♠. If these cards were all of one suit, it would be called a royal flush, which is the best possible straight flush.

Brush: An employee of a casino or card room who assists the players in getting seated, changing tables, and accommodating the players.

Bug: The Joker. A wild card which is most commonly used as another ace or as any card in a straight or flush.

Bull the Game: When a very aggressive player bets, raises and re-raises, often with marginal cards, other players refer to him or her as "bulling the game."

Bullet: Another name for an ace. Other terms for an ace are "Point" or "Rocket." When a player says he has "Pocket Rockets," he has a pair of aces.

Burn and Turn: To discard the top card and deal the next card(s) to the players, or in Hold 'Em, to place them in the center of the table. "Burn and turn" has developed as a deterrent against a player who would mark the cards. The second card is hidden by the top card. When the top card is discarded, the second card is dealt.

Burn Card: The top card that is discarded.

Busted Hand: A worthless hand. When a player is drawing at a straight or a flush and doesn't make it, that hand is called a "busted hand."

Button: An object to indicate who is the dealer or the designated dealer. It passes clockwise from player to player around the table. The effect of the button is to allow each player to be the dealer or the designated dealer. In Hold 'Em games, the dealer is the last to act (except for the blind hands before the flop).

Button Games: Some games, like all the Hold 'Em games, are button games.

Buy-in: The minimum amount of money required to enter a game. The higher the limit (or the blinds in a pot-limit or a no-limit game), usually the higher the buy-in required.

Call: Money placed in the pot to match a bet or raise.

Call Down: Taking a passive role by simply matching the bets of other players.

Calling Station: A term for a player who will call almost any bet but will seldom bet. A "calling station" is usually a conservative player who is cautious in his betting strategies.

Cap Off: Most house rules allow only a certain number of raises, usually three. To cap off means to place the final raise.

Cards Speak: A form of High-Low poker where the cards are placed face up at the conclusion of the hand and the value of the hands are read. "Cards speak" is contrasted with the player "declaring" one way or both ways (high and low). Obviously, the cards do not "speak" but are rather read.

Case Card: The last card of a particular rank left in the deck. If you need a six to complete a straight and you have noted that three sixes have appeared in other hands, you are drawing for the "case card."

Catch Perfect: In a longshot draw, when the player catches the exact card he needs. For instance, this could be the case card or an inside straight draw.

Center Dealer: In casinos and card rooms, center dealers are the rule. They shuffle and deal the cards, control the game, make change, declare the winner and deliver the pot.

Change Gears: When a player wants to confuse the other players, he will "change gears," or change his style of play. If he has been being very aggressive, raising and/or re-raising, he could become quite conservative in hand selection and betting strategies.

Chase: Trying to beat a hand that is better than yours. Chasing is also termed "going uphill" or "running him down."

Check: An action or spoken word to indicate the player does not wish to bet.

Checks: Chips.

Check Blind: This is an action some players will take when "under the gun." It means they check without looking at the next card or cards when they are first to act.

Check-raise: To check and then raise when the action gets back around. Sometimes there are rules against this, especially in home games. It is a powerful tool, and check-raising can intimidate some players.

Chip Runner: An employee of the casino or card room who assists the players in obtaining chips.

Chips: Plastic or clay objects of different colors to represent money.

Common Card: A card or cards placed face up in the center that can be used by all the players. All Hold 'Em games have common cards. Occasionally, in a Seven-Card Stud game, when there are more players than cards left to be distributed, the house rules can call for a common card to be placed in the center. It can be a very interesting development.

Complete Bluff: A bet that is made with a totally worthless hand. The bettor has no chance to win if called.

Concealed Pair: A pair where both cards are face down in either Seven-Card Stud or Texas Hold 'Em. A concealed pair is also called a "pair in the pocket."

Cowboy: Another name for the king.

Cripple the Deck: When you have such a good hand that no one is likely to beat you. In a Texas Hold 'Em game, you might flop a high full house or four of a kind. Conventional wisdom is usually not to bet immediately, hopefully allowing the others to catch up somewhat so they will call down your powerhouse hand.

Crying Call: To make a call when you have very little chance to win the pot. Usually this is done when the pot is large and you have just a slight suspicion that the bettor is bluffing.

Culling: A way of cheating that arranges the good cards in such a fashion that they are dealt to a certain person.

Dark Bet: To bet without looking at your hand. This is the opposite of checking blind. I guess the idea is to encourage competitors to call.

Dead Hand: A hand that has been fouled with too many or too few cards. This hand cannot be played.

Dealer's Choice: A poker game where the dealer chooses what game to play. In some games any kind of poker game can be called by the dealer.

Other games restrict the games to either the Hold 'Em games or to stud games or to draw games.

Declare: A form of High-Low poker where each person must declare which way his hand will play. A person can choose low, high or both ways. See *Cards Speak*.

Designated Dealer: When the game has a center dealer, a button is used to remind everyone which player is the last to receive cards or is acting as the dealer. In all Hold 'Em games, the designated dealer is the last to act on each betting round.

Dog: See *Big Dog*. This is the hand that is the opposite of the favorite.

Door Card: The first card dealt face up in stud poker.

Double Belly-buster Draw: A situation where one of two cards will make an inside straight. In Texas Hold 'Em, if you have J♦-5♦ and the flop comes 7♠-8♦-9♥, any six or ten will give you a straight. A double belly-buster has the same probabilities as an open-ended straight draw.

Double-pop: After a bet is made and another person raises it, when the second player re-raises that raise is called the "double-pop."

Down to the Green: The color of the table covering on poker tables is usually green. When a player has gone all in or put all his chips in, he is "down to the green."

Draw Hand: With more cards yet to come, a draw hand is an incomplete hand. This term usually refers to a flush or straight draw. In contrast, a "made hand" is a hand that is as good as it is likely to get.

Drawing Dead: Drawing at a hand when even if you make it, you cannot possibly win. Suppose you have a full house on fifth street in a Seven-Card Stud game and another person has already made a straight flush. There are two cards yet to come and there are no two cards that the first person can catch that will make him a winner. That straight flush is just too powerful. The person with the full house is "drawing dead."

Draw Out: When one person starts in the lead but another improves his hand and wins the pot. This often causes players to snip at each other and cast aspersions on how other people play the game.

Early, Middle and Late Position: Refers to the different positions during a hand. Early positions are the first three (two in stud games) players to act, middle positions are the next three or four (two or three in stud) and late positions are those remaining closest to the button.

Edge: An advantage that one player has over another. It can be a slight edge or a huge edge. Good players are always trying to calculate what edge they happen to have.

Exposed Pair: An exposed pair, as opposed to a split pair or a hidden pair, is on the board for all to see.

Family Pot: A pot where everyone at the table is involved.

Playing Fast: Playing a hand as aggressively as possible, betting and/or raising at every opportunity.

Fifth Street: In Hold 'Em, the last community card exposed. In stud, the fifth card dealt. In a structured Seven-Card Stud game, fifth street is where the bets double.

Fish: An easy player.

Floorman: The person in charge of a card room. He or she has the authority to resolve disputes.

Flop: In all the Hold 'Em games, the flop is the three community cards placed face up by the dealer. The flop also consists of the fourth street card and the fifth street card, also placed face up.

Flopping a Set: In Hold 'Em, when you have a pair in the hole and one of your cards comes on the flop. Usually a very good situation.

Flush: Five cards of one suit.

Fold: To withdraw from the action, to discard your cards.

Forced Bet: In some games, especially where there is neither an ante nor blinds, the person with either the lowest card or the highest card is forced to place the first bet.

Four-flush: Four cards of one suit.

Fourth Street: In Hold 'Em, the fourth community card exposed by the dealer. In Stud, the fourth card dealt.

Free Card: Everyone gets a card when no one bets during a betting round.

Full House: Three of a kind and a pair. Q♥-Q♠-Q♣-8♥-8♦

Getting a Hand Cracked: When a big hand is beaten by someone who drew out on the big hand. See also *Draw Out*.

Going to the Movies: A way to detect if a deck of cards is marked. See also *Riffling*.

Go Uphill: To chase or try to outdraw a better hand. See also *Chase*.

Gut Shot: An inside straight draw. See *Belly-Buster Straight Draw*.

Grifter: A cheat.

Heads-up: When two players compete for the pot. When this happens, the limit on the number of raises is removed. The two players can raise each other as long as they have money.

High Roller: A player who plays big stakes.

Hole Card(s): The card or cards that are dealt face down.

Hold-Out Artist: A cheater who hides a card or cards to use later in the game.

Hook: Another name for a jack. The name comes from the shape of the J. Another name commonly used is "fishhook."

Ignorant End of a Straight: The lower end of a straight in a game that has community cards. Also called the idiot end of the straight. Suppose these cards are the community cards: 7♦-8♣-9♥. The ignorant end would be the five-six. The nut straight would be the ten-jack.

Implied Odds: The ratio of the total amount of money a player expects to win if he makes his hand against the amount he must invest to continue in the hand.

In the Lead: According to the house rules, this is the player who starts the action. Usually he can check or bet.

In the Middle: A player caught between the bettor and a potential raiser. A tough place to be.

In the Pocket: Hole cards in stud and Hold 'Em games.

Jam: A pot where several players are raising.

Joker: A wild card used in some poker games. See also *Bug*.

Kibitzer: A spectator, usually one who is making comments on the play.

Kicker: In Texas Hold 'Em, when one of your hole cards is paired on the board, your other hole card is your kicker.

Kicker Trouble: When you have a weak kicker to go with your pair. Suppose you have these cards: A♥-7♥. The flop comes: A♣-8♦-J♦. This is good news and bad news. You have flopped the top pair, which is good. You have kicker trouble which is bad. Anyone else who is also playing an ace is likely to have a better kicker. That means you lose. There could be even more bad news if you should pair your kicker, giving you two pairs but also making a straight for anyone playing a nine-ten.

Lead Bet: The bet placed by the first person who wishes to bet.

Leather Ass: Refers to a player who is patient and willing to sit for long periods waiting for the good hand.

Limp In: To call a bet, usually in late position with a very marginal hand.

Little Blind: The first and smallest of the blinds.

Live Straddle: When the player to the left of the blinds puts up an optional blind bet. He also has the option of raising again when the action gets back to him. Suppose you are in a Texas Hold 'Em game with two blinds of $2 and $4. If allowed by the house rules, the live straddle would be $8. If a second live straddle was allowed, that would be $16. A live straddle is usually made by people who are on a rush, feel lucky or like to gamble. The disadvantage of a live straddle is that player's position is poor. He will have to act before most of the other players. A live straddle or two certainly does liven up the game.

Local: Usually refers to a Las Vegas resident, but it could also refer to anyone who plays in a casino/card room on a regular basis. The locals are usually pretty good players who feed off the tourists.

Lock: A hand that cannot lose. Also called the "mortal nuts."

Looking Down His Throat: Knowing that you can't be beat. This is a very nice place to be. It doesn't happen often, but it helps make your stack of chips look good.

Loose Player: A player who gets involved with a lot of hands.

Mechanic: A cheat who is skillful with the cards and can manipulate the cards to deal himself or another a good hand. A good mechanic is almost impossible to spot.

Miss the Flop: When your two cards in any Hold 'Em game do not correlate with the flop.

Muck: The discards. These are collected and piled in front of the dealer.

Nut Player: A very tight player who plays only the best hands.

Nuts: The best hand possible at that point.

Off-suit: In Hold 'Em, hole cards that are not of the same suit. An example is K♠-Q♣.

Omaha: A form of Hold 'Em where each player is dealt four cards. The player *has* to use two of those cards in his final five cards. This game is often played as High/Low split with an eight qualifier. The eight qualifier means the player must have five cards, all of eight and under, to qualify for low. The ace is considered both a low and high card.

On Board: The face-up cards in a poker game that are community cards.

On the Button: The person who is the designated dealer.

On the Come: Not a complete hand. Many players bet "on the come." Suppose you have these cards in a Seven-Card Stud game: 4♥-Q♥ K♥-7♥. You are "on the come" for a heart flush.

On the Rail: Someone watching a poker game.

On Tilt: A term referring to the emotional state of a player who is playing badly. Usually going "on tilt" results from anger over a bad beat or some verbal comment made by another player. Typical reactions are betting or calling with poor cards, throwing cards at the dealer and making derogatory remarks about the dealer or another player. Good players like to see another player go on tilt because that means he could start playing poorly and losing money.

Open-end Straight: Four consecutive cards. See also *Belly-Buster Straight Draw*.

Outs: The cards that can help your hand. In a Texas Hold 'Em game where you hold two clubs and two more clubs appear on the flop, you have nine "outs" in clubs. Any one of nine clubs will give you a flush. Don't make the mistake of thinking that if one of the "Outs" comes that you will have an automatic winner. It just ain't so.

Overcall: To call a bet after another player has already called. An overcall should be done with great care.

Overcard: The card held by a person in the hole that is higher than the cards on board.

Overpair: In Hold 'Em, a pair in the pocket that is higher than any card on the board. Suppose you have a pair of tens in the pocket and the flop is 9♣-7♦-2♥. Your pair of tens is an overpair.

Paint: A face card. The expression is usually used in a lowball game, where a paint is an undesirable card.

Pass: To check if no one has bet or to fold if someone has bet.

Picked Off: To get called when you are bluffing. Getting picked off in a low-limit game is very common.

Piece of Cheese: Can refer to an easy play or to a bad hand.

Pigeon: An easy player. These players are the kind experienced players are looking for. See also *Sucker*.

Play-back: A raise or a re-raise.

Play Behind: When playing in a table stakes game a player may announce that he is bringing out more money from his pocket. He announces that he is playing behind a certain amount of money. The usual rule is the player must not have looked at his hand before he does this.

Playing Over: When a player temporarily leaves his seat and another player will sit in until the first player returns. The new player must use his own chips. This commonly happens when the card room is crowded or a player leaves to eat dinner.

Porch: The up cards in a stud game.

Pot: The money in the center of the table which is being contested.

Pot Odds: The amount of money in the pot compared to the amount of money necessary to call. This is an important concept to master. If the bet is five dollars and you have a draw hand that has a one in four chance of improving, and if there is more than twenty dollars in the pot, the pot odds are favorable. See also *Implied Odds*.

Power Bet: To bet a hand very strongly.

Premium Hands: The best possible starting hands. These are usually raising hands but not always. For instance, this hand is a premium hand in Seven-Card Stud, High/Low Split, but I don't consider it a raising hand: 3♣-4♠-5♠. With that hand, I want as many people in the pot as possible. There is a lot of potential to win both ways with a good low and either a flush or a straight for high.

Prop Player: Also called Proposition Player. This player is employed by the casino or card room. He or she props the game in the sense they help a game get started or help keep one going if players leave. A "prop player" plays with his own money but gets a salary from the house. Contrast this with the Shill.

Puppy Feet: Another name for the suit of clubs.

Put a Play On: To attempt to win or increase the amount won by out-maneuvering an opponent.

Rags: Poor cards.

Raise: The action of placing more money in the pot than the initial bettor.

Rake: The percentage of the pot taken by the casino or house.

Rammer-jammer: An aggressive person who raises a lot.

Rat Hole: To take money or chips off the table during play. This is against the rules and customs of poker. The theory is that one should leave the money or chips on the table so that the losers have a chance to win it back.

Read: Attempt to guess what cards an opponent has.

Represent: Attempt to make an opponent believe you have a hand that you don't have. See also *Bluff*.

Ribbon Clerk: A small-time gambler.

Riffling: Taking a deck of cards and rapidly reviewing the whole deck.

Ring Game: A poker game with all the seats taken. Can also refer to a regular action game as opposed to a tournament game.

River Card: The last card dealt in a Hold 'Em game.

Rock: A conservative player.

Rolled-up: In Seven-Card Stud, when the first three cards dealt make trips.

Rush: A winning streak. Also called a heater.

Sandbag: Slow-playing a good hand with the intention of raising or check-raising later. The idea is to conceal the strength of the hand until more money is in the pot.

Scared Money: Money that a player uses that should be used to feed the family. He is afraid to lose that money. Betting scared money is a very bad policy.

Scoop: To win both ends in a High-Low game. Also known as *Sweep*.

Second Button: The second highest possible pair in a Texas Hold 'Em game. For instance, you have this hand: 9♣-T♣. The flop is K♦-T♠-2♥. You have the second button.

Second Nut Hand: The second best possible hand.

Semi-bluff: A bluffing play when there are some outs that could win the pot for you if your draw comes in. This is considered a good play under certain circumstances.

Set: Three of a kind, also known as trips.

Shill: A house player who plays with house money. The purpose of a shill is help get a game started or keep a game going. See also *Prop Player*.

Short-handed Game: A game not full. A different playing and betting philosophy should be employed in a short-handed game.

Showdown: The action of laying the cards face up to determine who will win the pot.

Side Pots: When one or more players go all in, that is put all their available money into the pot, the other active players can continue to wager. Their wagers go into the side pot or pots.

Sixth Street: The sixth card dealt in stud.

Slow-play: To let other players take the lead in betting. This is comparable to *Sandbagging*.

Snapped Off: To get a good hand beaten. See also *Draw Out* and *Getting a Hand Cracked*.

Solid Player: A strong all-around player. Certainly a player to be respected.

Speeding Around: Applies to a loose player who doesn't know what he is doing. Quite often he is betting and/or raising without really knowing why he is doing it.

Split Openers: Occasionally, in a jacks or better game of Five-Card Draw, a player who opens the betting may choose to draw to a straight or flush. In so doing, he might have to divide his opening pair, such as a pair of kings. The player announces his splitting action and places one of his kings face down on the table under an object, usually a chip. When the hand is completed, the opener shows that he had a pair of kings, thus qualifying him to open the betting.

Split Pair: A pair in stud with one card up and the other down.

Spread Limits: One form of betting in which any amount of money between certain limits can be wagered. If the game is a $1 to $10 game, any amount from $1 to $10 may be bet. See *Structured Limits*.

Standing Pat: The term used to define the action of not drawing any cards in a Five-Card Draw game.

Stay: To call or raise.

Steal Position: The next to last or last position. The reason that name evolved was because one of those players has the best position to steal the blinds. If no one has raised, one of these two players will often attempt to either win the blinds right then or force them into putting more money into the pot while in terrible position.

Straight: Any five cards in consecutive numerical value in at least two different suits.

Straight Flush: Any five cards in consecutive numerical value in only one suit.

Street: A term that defines which round of cards is being dealt. Third Street, for example, refers to the third card dealt.

String Bet: An illegal way of betting. A legal bet has to be made in one motion. A string bet is when a player makes a partial bet and watches for a reaction from the other players. If he gets the reaction he wants, he will complete the bet or raise. A string bet is consider unethical.

Stripper: A derivation of Pineapple Hold 'Em where three cards are dealt to each player and one card is discarded before the community cards are placed on the table.

Structured Limits: A form of betting in which a person can only bet a fixed amount. For instance: A $3–$6 game will allow only the $3 bet in the early betting round and a $6 bet in the later rounds. The later rounds of betting are always double the early rounds.

Sucker: A player who likes to play a lot of hands. He plays hands that should not be played. See also *Pigeon* and *Turkey*.

Sweep: To win both the high and low portions of the pot in a high/low split game. Also called a Hover.

Table Stakes: This is a rule that allows only the money on the table to be at risk. The player cannot dig into his pocket for more money during the course of a hand.

Tap: Going all in. See also *Down to the Green*.

Tell: A clue that reveals what a player has in his hand. Tells are important and usually profitable discoveries. Be aware that most of us display one or more tells. Try to eliminate any tell that you might have.

Third Street: In stud, the third card dealt.

Tied On: When your hand is good enough to play it to the end. Suppose you have the nut flush draw in a Texas Hold 'Em game. Usually the hand is tied on until after the fifth street card.

Tight Player: A person who plays only the premium hands. See also *rock*.

Toke: A tip. Most often given to the dealer. However, most places allow other service personnel to accept tokes.

Top Pair: In Hold 'Em, when the highest card on the board matches one of your hole cards.

Trips: Another name for three of a kind.

Turkey: A sucker. See also *Pigeon* and *Sucker*.

Turn Card: In the Hold 'Em family of games, the turn card is the fourth card exposed.

Underfull: A full house that is not the biggest possible full house. An underfull can be an expensive hand to get shown down.

Under the Gun: The first player to act.

Welcher: A player who fails to pay a debt. Unfortunately, there are these kinds of people hanging around poker games. Beware.

Wheel: See *Bicycle*.

Wild Cards: The cards so designated can be used to form pairs, straights, flushes, etc. See *Bug*.

Wired Pair: When the first two cards dealt to you are a pair.

INDEX

You can order other books on poker by Andy Nelson using this order form. If you do not like the books for any reason, return them and your money will be refunded.

Poker: 101 Ways to Win $17.95 (paperback)
   This 226-page book contains hints, tips, and strategies for winning presented in a series of short, readable chapters—perfect for a quick refresher before a casual Friday night game or an evening at the casino.

The books listed below, all well-received by the poker community, are 80 pages and priced at $8.95 each.

- *Poker: Hold 'Em, Book One*
- *Poker: Hold 'Em, Intermediate*
- *Poker: Hold 'Em, Advanced*
- *Poker: Omaha, High/Low Split, Book One*
- *Poker: Omaha, High/Low Split, Intermediate*
- *Poker: Seven Ways to Win*
- *Poker: Seven More Ways to Win*
- *Poker: Seven-Card Stud, High/Low Split, Book One*
- *Poker: Seven-Card Stud, High/Low Split, Intermediate*

Name _____

Address _____

City, State, & Zip _____

Make check payable to: PokerBook Press

Send to: PokerBook Press, PO Box 17851, Boulder, CO 80308

Please add $2.50 shipping and handling for the first book and 75 cents for each additional book. (We try to ship the next day, but sometimes the mail takes more than two weeks for delivery. Thanks!)

PLEASE NOTE: The books advertised here are not available through Perigee Books or The Berkley Publishing Group, which cannot accept responsibility for order fulfillment, guarantees offered by PokerBook Press, or for returns.